POSITIVE QUOTES
for
Every Day

PATRICIA LORENZ

Publications International, Ltd.

Patricia Lorenz is an art-of-living writer and speaker and the author of a dozen books, including *Life's Too Short to Fold Your Underwear* and *The 5 Things We Need to Be Happy*. She has written for numerous magazines and newspapers and has stories in more than 50 of the *Chicken Soup for the Soul* books. Patricia raised four children in Wisconsin (mostly as a single parent) and now lives in Florida, where she's following her dreams while she's still awake. Find Patricia at www.PatriciaLorenz.com.

Louis Weber, CEO
Publications International, Ltd.
7373 North Cicero Avenue
Lincolnwood, Illinois 60712

Permission is never granted for commercial purposes.

ISBN-13: 978-1-4508-0292-5
ISBN-10: 1-4508-0292-3

Manufactured in China.

8 7 6 5 4 3 2 1

Library of Congress Control Number: 2010924816

Make Each Day Sizzle

*I*magine yourself at an elegant cocktail party among the guests, overhearing their conversations. Now imagine a guest list of dozens of people so spectacular in their intelligence, thoughtfulness, and creative abilities that it boggles your mind to the point where you can hardly speak.

Why, there's Thomas Edison, Henry Ford, and Albert Einstein over in the corner discussing the effect of industry on the environment. On the other side of the room, the Reverend Martin Luther King Jr., Norman Vincent Peale, and Mother Teresa are carrying on a spirited dialogue. They are amazed by how much they have in common.

In the center of the room, Arnold Palmer, Lee Trevino, and Michael Jordan are discussing the finer points of the game of golf. Nearby, John Keats, William Shakespeare, and Carl Sandburg discuss the merits of free verse as Theodore Roosevelt, Robert F. Kennedy, and Abraham Lincoln hammer out a plan to attack the problems that plague the world.

Your head is spinning. Which of these amazing people do you introduce yourself to first? Anne Frank? Booker T. Washington? Mark Twain? Henry David Thoreau? You're desperate to meet and learn from all of them.

3

Relax. It's all here, in this book—a collection of the greatest words from some of the world's most thoughtful, creative people.

Elaborating on the words of these inspired people was daunting at first. How could I even begin to write about the words of such geniuses? But then I decided it might be helpful for a nongenius such as myself to ponder what the truly brilliant had to say, and then put their ideas into a reflection that would carry their thoughts into our own lives. And what better way to honor these individuals than by suggesting a down-to-earth action for each day of the year based on their words?

And this is it, my friends: famous quotes to soothe, encourage, and inspire us. These quotes are revered because of their timelessness and their timeliness. Such words can add unfathomable vibrancy to our own lives. Someday perhaps the rest of us will be inspired by a famous quote written by you.

I always tell my writing students, "In order to be a good writer, you must unzip your soul and expose your foibles." There, I made my own quote. Unzipping my soul is what I've tried to do in this book. Creating it has been a joy rather than a chore, and I hope it shows.

Patricia Lorenz

Happy New Year

*"The best thing about the future is that
it comes only one day at a time."*

Abraham Lincoln

*I*sn't it exciting to have a whole new year spread out before us? We have all those days to fill exactly as we want and to accomplish something worthwhile. Look at last year's calendar and see all the things you did, places you visited, social engagements you participated in, and work you accomplished. It's a good thing we start each year with a clean slate. We don't want to know all the things we're going to do this year and all the work that we will accomplish. If we did, it would be daunting; we might give up before we started. But one day at a time—we can do that.

Today I will start fresh. I will accomplish a little and reflect on it this evening. I will begin to break one bad habit and adopt one good one. You too? Bravo! Let's get started.

Walk on the Wild Side

"If we listened to our intellect, we'd never have a love affair. We'd never have a friendship. We'd never go into business, because we'd be too cynical. Well, that's nonsense. You've got to jump off cliffs all the time and build your wings on the way down."

Annie Dillard

We wear seat belts, sunscreen, and helmets. We exercise and try to eat right. But sometimes we need to be spontaneous and silly. We need to blow kazoos, dance with our inner rubber chicken, and strut like turkeys. Life is short—make time to enjoy it.

Today I will make reservations for something unusual—perhaps a belly-dancing class or a trip to the circus with my grandchildren.

Take Another Look

"Just because something doesn't do what you planned it to do doesn't mean it's useless."

Thomas Alva Edison

Creativity is a wonderful thing. The ability to put things to good use is a talent—a gift to be treasured and used daily. A piece of fabric found at a rummage sale can be turned into stunning curtains for the bathroom. A couple of bolts, nuts, screws, planks of wood, and beach debris can form an amazing sculpture. Celebrate the making of something new.

Today I will take a new look at something I was going to toss, and I will try to find a use for it.

A Positive Outlook

"We didn't lose the game; we just ran out of time."

Vince Lombardi

When Vince Lombardi was the Green Bay Packers coach, he amassed a stunning 98–30–4 record and collected six division titles, five NFL championships, and two Super Bowl victories. Lombardi drilled his players and constantly worked to come up with new strategies. His teams were successful because Lombardi's positive attitude radiated to his players. They were relentless, and nothing discouraged them.

Today I will strive to be a winner. I will not make excuses to get out of exercising. I will just get on my bike, and before I know it, I will have ridden ten miles.

A Bowl of Cherries with Pits

"Some people are always grumbling because roses have thorns; I am thankful that thorns have roses."

Alphonse Karr

*L*ife is full of glorious things with not-so-savory appendages. Collies are sweet and lovable...but why does my best friend have to come with such smelly poop to scoop? The love of my life takes my breath away, but even he snores, picks his teeth, and complains about my shopping habits. The good comes hand-in-hand with the bad. Which part are you focusing on?

Today I will focus on my love's positive characteristics—his generosity, his willingness to spend time with my family, his loyalty. I will overlook the time he spends watching sports on TV.

Getting Ready

*"Great opportunities come to all, but many
do not know they have met them."*

A. E. Dunning

*A*ll the great individuals of the world became great because they were open to (and seized) opportunities rather than shrinking from them. It is easier and safer to say no, but if we say yes, each opportunity brings more acquaintances and more opportunities.

Today I will be open to each and every opportunity that comes my way.

Me, Myself, and I

"My grandfather once told me that there were two kinds of people: Those who do the work, and those who take the credit. He told me to try to be in the first group; there was much less competition."

Indira Gandhi

I once knew a man named Henry who rented the ballroom at an exclusive club for his 70th birthday party. His wife took care of the invitations and arranged for the food, music, and flowers. Once the party was under way, Henry began his speech: "I always wanted to throw a big party when I turned 70, and I'm so glad I was able to pull it off." He did not thank his wife during his speech; rather, he prattled on and on about his achievements. If this is how he treats his wife, I do not even want to know how he treats his employees or coworkers.

Today I will work hard, and I will acknowledge the work of others.

Encouragement

"Correction does much, but encouragement does more."

Johann Wolfgang von Goethe

I struggle and I strive. I do it wrong. I'm corrected in front of the class. I wither and I grow silent. The next day I struggle more, but this time I ask for help. I practice. Again, I do it wrong. Then someone notices my determination, my willingness to keep going. "You've almost got it. Don't give up," they say. The next day, more struggles, more striving, but I work hard, promising myself I will get it. "Look! You're getting closer. I am proud of you. You can do it." And finally, I do. The encouraging voice makes me feel like I can walk on water.

Today I will offer someone an encouraging word, no matter how far they are from completing a project.

Kindness Makes the World a Better Place

*"Three things in human life are important.
The first is to be kind. The second is to
be kind. The third is to be kind."*

Henry James

Kind. It's such a simple word. It's the goodness that trickles from our very nature. Life jades us, stresses us, and tempts us to be mean, crabby, and inconsiderate. But kindness is still in there. We can be kind. *Kind*—it may be the best word of all.

Today, no matter how tired, cranky, stressed, or irrational I may feel, I will choose to be kind.

Picking Up Good Habits

"We are what we repeatedly do. Excellence, then, is not an act but a habit."

Aristotle

Some specialists believe that it takes only 30 days to make a habit. Are you eager to start a healthy habit? Try walking a mile every day for one month. After one month it'll be a habit—you'll do it without even thinking. Add five blocks to that mile the second month, and do that for 30 days. Add five more blocks the next month, and before you know it, you'll be walking two miles every day. You'll be amazed at how great and energized you feel.

Today I will pay special attention to my habits, and I will make sure they are ones I am proud of.

Lead by Example

*"You can preach a better sermon with
your life than with your lips."*

Oliver Goldsmith

I admit it—my mind tends to wander during sermons. Things sink in better when I hear real-life stories about people who have solved problems their own unique way. Those priests, pastors, and rabbis who walk the walk and share true stories I can relate to—rather than fire and brimstone—are the ones who get through to me.

Today I will walk the walk—I will make sure my actions reflect my beliefs.

The Gift of Today

"Don't let yesterday use up too much of today."

Will Rogers

Yesterday is old news. Let it go. (Though if you spent yesterday in such a way that you hurt someone or messed something up...well, fix it. Then move on.) Today is today. It's a fresh, new, anything-can-happen day. Exercise, shower, look your best, and step out into the world. Today is yours.

I resolve to focus on today. If twinges of regret creep into my mind, I will quash them. Regret is a waste of time.

Reveal the Beauty

*"I saw the angel in the marble and
carved until I set him free."*

Michelangelo

*L*ook around you—at your home, your
neighborhood, or your community. Are
things as you would have them, or do you
wish they were different? Make small changes
to emphasize the beautiful. Does your home
environment help you feel hopeful, or is it dark
and rather dreary? If necessary, try repainting a
small area. Uncover the beauty around you.

**Today I will pinpoint something that needs
improvement, and I will get to work.**

Giving Back

*"We are cups, constantly and quietly being
filled. The trick is, knowing how to tip ourselves
over and let the beautiful stuff out."*

Ray Bradbury

It's count-your-blessings day. Do you have food in
your belly? Check. Do you have clothes on your
back? Check. Do you have a roof over your head?
Check. Do you have someone to love or care for?
Come on, family members, coworkers, neighbors,
and fellow church or club members all count.
Do you have a dream, a goal—something to look
forward to? If not, ponder one, plan for it, and
make it come true. Once you have all that you need
in life, it's time to give back. Make sure everybody
else you know and care about has all they need.

**Today I will reach out to a loved one who's going
through a difficult time.**

Healing

*"Our scientific power has outrun our spiritual power.
We have guided missiles and misguided men."*

Martin Luther King Jr.

Martin Luther King Jr. lived in a troubled, volatile time. Society was steeped in resentment and suspicion of others, and he called on everyone to love each other and work together for a better society. He changed our world, and today—on his birthday—we reflect on his life and express our gratitude for the strides that he made.

Today I will reflect on Martin Luther King Jr.'s work. I will feel the love, and I will do my part to spread it near and far.

January 16

Making Time for Beauty

"One ought, every day at least, to hear a little song, read a good poem, see a fine picture, and if it were possible, to speak a few reasonable words."

Johann Wolfgang von Goethe

Whether we live in a mansion overlooking an ocean or in a tenement house in a noisy city, we all have the ability to appreciate little things that can lift our spirits. Maybe we can take time to notice the beautiful sunshine; the majestic trees; or an amazing, starlit sky. Or perhaps we can refresh our spirits with a trip to a museum or the library. Sometimes it takes effort to find the beauty in our lives, but our refreshed outlook is well worth it.

Today I will look for and savor the beautiful.

Talk Is Cheap

"Well done is better than well said."

Benjamin Franklin

*E*veryone likes a good speech. Words, when put together carefully, can be beautiful and pleasing. The best speeches, however, are the ones that accompanied great accomplishments. If speeches are not accompanied by action, speeches are meaningless and forgotten.

Today I will resist any urge to boast. I will let my work speak for itself.

January 18

I Think I Can

***"Whether you think you can or think
you can't, you're right."***

Henry Ford

*M*ind over matter—it seems almost too easy,
but things really are that simple. If you go
into a project dreading it, sure of failure—surprise!
You will fail. But if you go into a project with a
playful, curious, hopeful attitude, you'll get there
because you believed in yourself and kept at it.

Today, I think I *can*.

Courage

*"I love the man that can smile in trouble,
that can gather strength from distress,
and grow brave by reflection."*

Thomas Paine

The truly inspiring people among us are not the ones who have it all. No, it's the wise ones—those who have struggled and can look back with satisfaction. Think of those who endured prison camps—or even wrongful imprisonment—and maintained their joy and hopefulness during such trying circumstances. They may have more of a right to bitterness than anyone, but because they endured with courage and hopefulness, they are truly beautiful.

Today I will face my struggles with courage and hopefulness.

January 20

Leading by Example

*"If you don't have the power to change yourself,
then nothing will change around you."*

Anwar Sadat

The most important role of parents and employers is to teach by example. Forget the shouts, directives, and orders—the "you'll do this or else" routines. Just lead quietly by example. Unless, of course, you want your kids or employees to be just like you when you're in a tyrannical, loud, aggressive mood. Of course you don't.

Today I will be patient even if all around me are losing their heads.

Absolutely

"Yes, I said, yes I will, yes."

James Joyce

*F*or years my philosophy of life has been *"Never* say no to an opportunity unless it's illegal or immoral." This philosophy solves all my decision-making problems. Many of us favor the same routine close to home and tend to say *no* when someone suggests something different to do. But if you adopt my philosophy, you don't have to ponder or make up excuses. You simply always say yes when someone suggests something new and different. Sure, there will be times when an offer conflicts with other plans, but something can usually be worked out. Yes! Say *yes!*

Today I will say yes to any new idea, plan, event, or adventure.

January 22

Enthusiasm Moves Mountains

*"The secret of genius is to carry the spirit
of the child into old age, which means
never losing your enthusiasm."*

Victor Hugo

For far too long I've been overwhelmed by the
amount of junk I've collected. When I moved
to Florida in 2004, I gave away, sold, or tossed
two-thirds of everything I owned. But after six
years in Florida, I did it again—filled every available
space to overflowing. But happily, *today* I found the
enthusiasm to really do something about this.

I walked from room to room, counting all the
shelves, drawers, and cupboards. One living room,
one bedroom, one office, one kitchen, six closets,
and a porch contain 176 storage spaces. I made a
chart listing each room and the spaces in each area.
During my survey of the house, I found a packet
of fun stickers in one drawer. Each day I will put a
sticker on the chart for each space I've organized. I
am again a child who is proud of her stickers!

I found four large cardboard boxes and labeled
them: *Donate, Give to Family* (heirlooms, keepsakes,
etc.), *Sell,* and *Trash.* I made a plan to clean three

spaces three times a week (Mondays, Wednesdays, Fridays). That's nine a week. In five months my home will be clutter-free, organized, and a much nicer, more relaxing space. I know this job will not be accomplished in a day, but I am so enthused about this project, I can hardly contain myself.

I have already begun my work with the living room; it is the easiest area because there are only four spaces where clutter can collect. In under an hour, I was nearly finished. I'm on my way!

Today I will muster enthusiasm for a task I typically dread. I will iron as though there is nothing else I would rather be doing.

January 23

Small or Great

*"Keep away from people who try to belittle your
ambitions. Small people always do that, but the really
great make you feel that you, too, can become great."*

Mark Twain

Really great people see potential everywhere
because there really *is* potential everywhere—
if you have the right attitude. If you're not
particularly interested in getting anywhere (or
having anyone around you get anywhere), it's easy
to just sit back, watch—and criticize. But if you
really want to get somewhere or do something,
there are means all around you! A petty person
might say, "Oh, that train—it is so loud, and it
blows disgusting exhaust everywhere." A great
person might say, "Oh, that train! It can get me to
California! How wonderful!" See the difference?

**Today I will look for the potential in everything
and everyone around me.**

Happiness Overflowing

"Fill the cup of happiness for others, and there will be enough overflowing to fill yours to the brim."

Rose Pastor Stokes

*M*ost of us are naturally givers *and* takers. When we see another in need, we yearn to help. We also have that basic instinct to survive, however, so we are takers as well. Wouldn't it be great if everyone in the world was a 90 percent giver and only a 10 percent taker? The love quotient in the universe would soar. There would be no more wars, and we'd all have plenty of work and plenty of food. We would be spending our lives making nice, and our own lives would be the better for it.

Today I will focus on others and feel the love.

January 25

The Passion of Life

"In the human heart new passions are forever being born; the overthrow of one almost always means the rise of another."

François de la Rochefoucauld

I love the word *passion.* Just think of all the things we're passionate about. I am passionate about humor and trying to get the world healthier by laughing more. I'm passionate about living my life in a happy, low-stress way. I'm passionate about being able to swim every day if I want to, and it must be outdoors in warm weather under sunny skies. I'm passionate about traveling and meeting new people, and about painting jars and plates and giving them away.

Today I will focus on one passion and go after a project with gusto.

The Gift of Imagination

"Imagination is everything. It is the preview of life's coming attractions."
Albert Einstein

*B*ig blankets, warm summer nights, and a sky full of stars are the perfect setting for lying on the grass, watching for shooting stars, and thinking up stuff. Under these circumstances, it is easy to just let our imaginations run wild. Our imaginations are among our greatest gifts. The trouble is, many of us never exercise our imaginations. We just live our lives as though our present world is the best it can be. Deep down, though, we know it can be better. It will just take a little imagination—and work—on our part.

Today I will give my imagination free rein.

When I Grow Up...

"Keep true to the dreams of thy youth."

Friedrich von Schiller

Sometimes it takes a lifetime to follow our dreams. We get sidetracked. Maybe we fall in love and before we know it, we're married with three children. Then the focus is all on work, work, work, and save, save, save. Perhaps some of us are in our 50s, and we're just now trying to decide how to spend the rest of our lives. Think back on the dreams of your childhood. Did you want to be an artist? Or perhaps own your own bakery with a specialty in wedding cakes? Did you want to take up scuba diving or learn to pilot your own plane? Don't let anything hold you back. It is never too late to put a dream into motion.

Today I will reflect on my life dreams and make progress toward at least one of them.

Strength of Character

"Great things are not accomplished by those who yield to trends and fads and popular opinion."

Jack Kerouac

Trends, fads, and popular opinion are some of the strongest forces in our society. They are enticing, and they are powerful. If we don't stay grounded by reflection, it is easy to be swept up in it all. Trends and fads are innocent and harmless in moderation—we just need to make sure there is more to our lives.

Today I will put down the celebrity magazine or walk away from reality TV and focus on something that will truly improve my quality of life. Maybe I will take a walk with a friend or crack open an enlightening classic.

The Ties That Bind

"The best thing to hold onto in life is each other."

Audrey Hepburn

Humans are social creatures. We can have all the money and the finest things in the world, but if we have no loved ones to share and enjoy it with, we will likely feel empty and alone. Specialists advise that many and varied social connections keep us healthier and happier; they expand our minds and invigorate us. Relationships require a lot of give and take, and sometimes we may feel as if we would be better off alone. We would not be, though. Often—even after a considerable disagreement—once we have talked it out, our bond is stronger than ever.

Today I will reach out—whether it's to that friend I talk to every week or an acquaintance with whom I've only recently connected.

Principles

*"A people that values its privileges above
its principles soon loses both."*

Dwight D. Eisenhower

*M*any of us are so used to our privileges that we take them for granted. A warm house is a privilege. Having a government that actually cares about keeping people safe and keeping the streets clean and reasonably repaired is a privilege. Most people in the world have none of these privileges. We gained these privileges because previous generations established a society based on freedom and justice. It now falls to us to preserve these privileges by having high ideals—by spending wisely and valuing freedom, hard work, and integrity.

At brunch today, I will acknowledge the waitress's hard work by leaving her a bigger tip, then I will forgo the privilege of a midafternoon tea-and-cookie at the local bakery.

January 31

Taking Chances

"One doesn't discover new lands without consenting to lose sight of the shore for a very long time."

André Gide

*L*eaving home (or just leaving our comfort zone) is difficult. We are sure to feel lost at times. This is the only way to grow, though. If we never make ourselves uncomfortable, we never change or discover new things. Change is part of life, and we must embrace it. Besides, sometimes we feel most at home only after feeling very lost. We are smarter and more aware of what's around us, so we feel strong, confident, and secure.

If I find myself feeling scared and unsure today, I will collect myself and just go for it. I will not let fear keep me from growing.

I Think I Can, I Think I Can

"Clear your mind of can't."

Samuel Johnson

The last time I replaced my watchband, the store would not put it on my watch for me. The salesclerk instructed me to just use a knife to hold the spring-loaded pin as I put the new band in place. After I got home, I tried and tried, but each time, the pin would slip. I became frustrated. *I can't do this—maybe my fingers aren't as nimble as they used to be,* I whined to myself. After some deep breaths, I resolved to keep trying. I tried again and again. Finally, the little pin slipped into place. Another dozen tries later, the second one slipped in. It was an invigorating feeling.

Today I will not give up, no matter what obstacles come my way. I will take deep breaths to clear my head, and I will forge ahead.

One Chance to Get It Right

"I expect to pass through this world but once.
Any good therefore that I can do, or any
kindness that I can show to my fellow-creature,
let me do it now. Let me not defer
or neglect it, for I shall not pass this way again."

Stephen Grellet

When you look back on your past, are there actions you regret? Most of us have them, and they take one of two forms: either something you wish you had not done, or something you wish you had done. Of the two, explaining the thing you wish you had not done is usually easier than explaining the thing you knew you should have done but didn't. The first can often be explained away by confusion, but the second can really only be laziness, selfishness, or fear. Take the passersby who see someone fall; all but one continues on their way because they're "in a hurry." The ones who continue on will likely feel a twinge of regret that they did not have the courage or decency to behave as the kind passerby did.

Today, if an opportunity to help presents itself, I will boldly step forward.

So Many Books

"A book lying idle on a shelf is wasted ammunition."

Henry Miller

*L*ike grains of salt in the saltshaker, there are so many books—all filled with varied information and insight. I wonder if I'll ever read even the ones I already own? What about the ones in the small library across the street? And what about the ones at the big library downtown, and at all the bookstores, and online, and the ones my friends have offered to share? I suppose the way to do it is the same way you eat an elephant: one bite at a time. One sentence, one paragraph, one page, one chapter—one book at a time.

Today I will begin to read the books I already own. Just think of the great conversations I'll be able to start!

Alone and Loving It

"Better be alone than in bad company."
Thomas Fuller

*M*ost of us can call to mind times when we were tempted to hang out with "bad company." Maybe they were people who tempted us to party excessively or not work as hard as we should. Maybe it was in school, when they were concentrating on escaping rather than focusing on their studies. Or maybe it was even later in life, when they were still concentrating on escaping rather than attending to their responsibilities. "Bad company" is generally composed of people who think too much of themselves and their own wants and needs, rather than being part of and improving a community. Though who is to say—maybe those high school burnouts are now pillars of their communities, and maybe the "bad company" you've run into recently will one day reshape their city or the world. It is certainly healthier to wish only good things for them.

Today if someone is polluting the air around me with their negativity, I will walk away, tune them out, or respond only with constructive comments.

One of a Kind

"Always be a first-rate version of yourself,
instead of a second-rate version of somebody else."
Judy Garland

ver hear these words, "I wish I was her"?
I want to holler, "No, you don't! Be glad
you're *you*. You're unique!" People who try to
consistently dress like a specific movie star or
mindlessly follow in their father's career footsteps
instead of utilizing their own inherent talents are
making huge mistakes. We each are unique, and we
have one life. Be yourself and make the most of
your specific assets.

**If I'm tempted to compare myself to someone else
today, I will think back over the past few days and
focus on something I can be proud of.**

Thanks to Fear

*"None but a coward dares to boast
that he has never known fear."*

Ferdinand Foch

Many times fear has shot my stress-level indicator up into the red zone. When my ex-husband took to drinking too much and became abusive, for instance. Or when my daughter was in the area hit by the California earthquake of 1989. Or when I moved to Florida and arrived 30 hours before the second of four hurricanes howled through my neighborhood that month. Anyone who claims to have never been afraid is a little off their rocker, a liar, or has not ventured very far off the beaten path.

Today I will reflect on the times in my past when I have been the most scared. I will think about what I learned from those events, and how they strengthened me.

Hearts Beating, Eyes Fluttering

*"Experience shows us that
love does not consist in gazing at each other
but in looking together in the same direction."*

Antoine de Saint-Exupéry

Did you ever sit across from the one you love and try to look into each other's eyes for any length of time? It's an exercise that usually dissolves into massive blinking, watering eyes, and fits of laughter. True love is a side-by-side thing, not an *in-your-face* thing. Walking together, holding hands, aiming for the same goals, all while respecting each one's individuality—that's true love. We don't need to stay transfixed on each other's pupils to see the depth of our love. We just need to look forward to similar things.

Today I will sit down with the love of my life and plan our next adventure.

43

Dream First, Plan Second

"Your vision will become clear only when you look into your heart. Who looks outside, dreams. Who looks inside, awakens."

Carl Jung

How do we look into our own heart? We sit in a quiet place and figure out if we are happy—if we are doing what we want to be doing. Do you take time to do that, or are you focused on the outside? Stop and search your heart—it is the only way to happiness and fulfillment. Do you love your job, or would you give anything to be doing something else? If so, what is that "something else"? Work toward that, whether it means finding a new job or staying at your current job and taking classes or joining a group. Find happiness—it is within your reach, and you will know the way if you stop to search within yourself.

Today I will close my eyes and look inside my heart. Am I doing what I want to be doing? Once I have reflected, I will jot down a concrete goal or two and begin working toward them.

Shoulders Back, Chin Up

"The fear of rejection is worse than rejection itself."

Nora Profit

*M*any of us modern humans have a tendency to overthink things. Take the guy who has always wanted to learn to paint but is afraid of being the worst student in the class. Or the woman who would love to make jewelry but is nervous about handling those crazy tools. Or the shy college student who steals looks at that girl in his economics class, but lacks the courage to just open his mouth and ask her if she wants to grab a cup of coffee sometime. What a bunch of scaredy-cats we are. What's the worst that could happen? We might fail or someone might say *no?* Well at least we tried and now we *know,* right? Life goes on. Plus, it's just as likely it could be the start of something great—once we take that first step, of course.

Today I will try something I've hesitated to do in the past. Perhaps I will enlist in that dance class—who cares if I have no rhythm at first? With practice, I know I will shine.

Let Small Things Roll Off Your Back

"You can tell the size of a man by the size of the thing that makes him mad."

Adlai Stevenson

What makes you mad? A long line at the post office? The restaurant messing up your order? Someone cutting you off in traffic? These things might be annoying, but they are small matters, aren't they? Perhaps a postal worker had an emergency and that office is short-handed today. Hasn't that happened at our workplaces before? Chalk it up to bad timing. The messed up order? The restaurant workers are human, and they make mistakes, just like the rest of us. The unpredictable car on the road? That one's a little harder, but it is possible the driver has never driven in that area before and is just flustered. Be understanding and forgiving—maybe someone will do the same for you one day.

Today, I will take a deep breath and be forgiving, no matter what small thing crosses my path. I will not lose my cool.

Friendship Funny Bones

*"We cannot really love anybody
with whom we never laugh."*

Agnes Repplier

For a few years after our friendship began,
my best friend and I didn't laugh with each
other that much. Her sense of humor is very
different from mine. Once I put plastic spiders in
her suitcase and on the shower floor in the room
we were sharing at a writer's conference. She didn't
seem to find my goofy sense of humor that funny.
But as the years went by, I think I finally earned
a soft spot in her heart. For my birthday last year,
she sent me a new rubber chicken in a box marked
"frozen seafood." There were also 100 teeny rubber
chickens tucked in the package for good measure.

**Today I will do something to make someone laugh.
Perhaps I will send a teeny rubber chicken to a
friend who least expects it.**

The Very Core of Life

*"Friendship is composed of
a single soul inhabiting two bodies."*

Aristotle

I adore, treasure, and rejoice in my friends. My best friend lives a thousand miles away in Washington, D.C. My best neighbor-friend is a snowbird, so she's only in Florida six months out of the year. Betsy is my best Wisconsinite-friend (I lived in Wisconsin for 24 years). Catherine is my sister who lives a block away, and there's nothing better than having a best sister-friend who lives so close. Friends are like air and light—essential.

Today I will think about my closest friends, choose one who is maybe going through a difficult time, and write a note telling her how thankful I am to have her in my life.

Loving Our Differences

"If you judge people, you have no time to love them."

Mother Teresa

Whom have you judged recently? The slacker at work whom everyone talks about? The celebrity who's splashed across the tabloids day after day? I know I used to have preconceived notions about bikers. They just always seemed suspect to me, with their tattoos, gruff voices, and roaring Harleys. But I recently learned that these are the same giant teddy bears who organize the Toys for Tots program in our town every year. Now I love them and feel lucky to have them in our community.

Today if I am tempted to judge someone, I will try to reach out to them instead.

February 14

Love Me Tender

*"Love is an act of endless forgiveness,
a tender look which becomes a habit."*

Peter Ustinov

I never knew about tender looks until I met Jack, the love of my life. With my first husband, I was busy looking after the kids, while he grew more and more focused on the bottle. My second husband never seemed to be around once we tied the knot. The boyfriend I had after that—well, I just knew deep inside that he was not "the one." Then, a dozen years after that breakup, Jack came along. Fun, caring, wonderful Jack. On the porch each morning as we sit across from each other, reading the paper, I feel his tender look as he turns pages. At parties, in the midst of rousing conversation with a bunch of neighbors, I feel that look. I know he loves me—truly loves me for me, despite my many faults. It is a beautiful, calming feeling.

I resolve to act lovingly today in all that I do.

Love Breeds Strength

*"Love conquers all things except
poverty and toothache."*

Mae West

*L*ove can get us through so much, can't it?
It may not conquer poverty and can
only ease a toothache so much, but ponder for a
moment the innumerable things that love *does*
conquer: The spouses who find the strength to
work through any problem because they are that
committed to making their union work. The parents
who forgive the wayward child again and again
because they will not lose the faith that has formed
out of their love. The child who takes the aging
parent in and lovingly and patiently tends to his or
her every need. We make these sacrifices again and
again—and the only explanation is love.

**Today I will lean on love to find the strength for
each and every task I face.**

Annie Fanny

"You grow up the day you have your
first real laugh—at yourself."

Ethel Barrymore

My mother always gave me a pair of red cotton underpants for Valentine's Day, including when I was in college and working as a cashier at a local grocery. That year, as a joke, she sewed a big white heart on the backside of the panties. A few weeks later, all the checkers and baggers took to calling me "Annie Fanny." "What's up with you guys?" I asked, as their giggles bounced off the walls. Later that same evening—as I was at home taking off my shoes—my roommate began laughing uproariously. "You can totally see your red panties with the white heart through your uniform!" she said. I wanted to die, but I couldn't help laughing too. The next day at work, all I could do was waltz right in: "Annie Fanny, reporting for duty!"

Today I will not hesitate to laugh at myself.
It's good for the heart, soul, mind, and body.

Star Light, Star Bright

"When it is dark enough, you can see the stars."
Ralph Waldo Emerson

When my youngest son was small, times were not easy. I was a struggling single mother, and he was just beginning to explore this wide world of ours. One day—on a whim—we bought two kits of stick-on, glow-in-the-dark stars. We were thrilled with the idea that we could go to sleep at night looking at the constellations on our ceilings. After studying the stars and their formations, we hopped from chair to chair to bed to chair, sticking big stars and little stars all over the ceilings of our bedrooms. Every night after that, the stars glowed like fireflies, lulling us into dreamland.

Today I will look on the bright side for the stars, even if cold, dreary weather dampens my mood. I will light a fire, make hot tea, or call a friend I haven't spoken to in a while.

The Blessing of Variety

"If you don't change what you are doing today, all of your tomorrows will look like yesterday."

Jim Rohn

What is your daily life like? Do you get up at the same time, go to work, come home, eat dinner, watch TV, go to bed, and then do it all over again the next day? Shaking up your routine is energizing and good for your brain.

Today I will do one thing to shake things up. Perhaps I will take a walk during lunch or ask a friend to grab a bite to eat.

Extinguish the Fire

*"The fire you kindle for your enemy
often burns you more than him."*

Chinese Proverb

It takes work and energy to remain enemies, doesn't it? Perhaps your enemy is a neighbor you don't like, a bully at school, a boss who is condescending or holds you back, a greedy relative, or a friend who betrayed you. Goodness, we can make an "enemy" out of almost anyone. Remember, one little snit does not an enemy make. Being in close quarters with other people breeds conflict, but we can summon the wisdom and compassion to resolve any problem. Deal with whatever set you off. Talk it out or send a written note, if necessary. Extinguish the fire that is burning you up inside, and move on. There are too few hours in the day as it is—don't waste any on unproductive resentment and revenge.

Today if someone hurts me, I will give myself two choices: Let it go, or confront the person and talk it out. I will not let a grudge burn me up inside.

Life Lessons

*"Always do right. This will gratify some
people and astonish the rest."*

Mark Twain

A bank teller once gave me $10 too much
when I cashed a check. I was a struggling
single parent living on less than $10,000 a year at
the time, so it would have been easy to rationalize
keeping the extra money. I did the right thing,
however; I didn't want the teller to get in trouble
just so I could have the few extra bucks. Several
people learned a good lesson that day—I learned
that it feels good to do the right thing no matter
what, the teller likely learned to be more careful,
and my kids (who were in the car at the time)
witnessed a teaching moment. I've always hoped
they got the message, and so far, it looks promising.

**I will make a special effort to do the right thing in
all the situations I face today.**

The Heart of the Matter

*"The history of every country begins
in the heart of a man or a woman."*

Willa Cather

When historians list the greatest leaders of all time, Abraham Lincoln is near the top of the list. Lincoln encountered many obstacles in his life—he had only one year of formal schooling, he failed in business, he lost many elections, one fiancée died, his wife suffered great mental and physical ailments, and only one of his four sons lived to adulthood. Lincoln's personal struggles gave him wisdom and the strong heart he needed to lead a young country through a time of great darkness.

Today I will research some articles about great leaders from history. I will figure out how I can put some of their ideals to work in my own life.

February 22

Peacefully Speaking

"There is no way to peace. Peace is the way."

A. J. Muste

A friend once told me that in her 25-plus years of marriage, she and her husband had never had an argument. My jaw dropped, and all my own tumultuous married years came flooding to mind. But I began to pay more attention when I was around this couple, and I realized she was not delusional. Peace permeates this couple's home. They are considerate and affectionate. I believe they will be one of those couples who are still holding hands and looking at each other with complete devotion on their 60th wedding anniversary. Peace is possible, and it starts with respect.

Today I will be respectful, and I will revel in the peace.

Growing a Child

"Treat people as if they were what they ought to be and you help them to become what they are capable of being."

Johann Wolfgang von Goethe

Grandmas tend to see only the good qualities in their grandchildren, don't they? My grandma always made me feel like there was no one she would rather spend time with. She delighted in being with me, out there on the porch, rocking in the doublewide swing. She hung on my every word—even during my awkward adolescent years, when my words were sometimes halting and unsure. I adored that woman. Now that I'm a grandma, I prefer to have each grandchild one at a time so I can give them what my grandma gave me: her precious time and undivided attention. Such attention builds a child's self-esteem, and confidence is the cornerstone of a life.

Today if I encounter someone who is struggling, I will make a special effort to encourage or compliment them.

The Life Cycle

"Age is mind over matter. If you don't mind, it doesn't matter."

Satchel Paige

I have heard that the seven stages of life are made up of spills, drills, thrills, bills, ills, pills, and wills. Sounds pretty awful except for the *thrills* part, doesn't it? *Spills* are for toddlers, *drills* for young children, *thrills* for teens and 20-somethings, *bills* for young couples and homeowners, *ills* for those in midlife, *pills* for folks in their 60s and up, and *wills* for the aged.

I refuse to live life this way. The older I get, the more I understand that there are no definite stages of life. All lives are different. We can see life as one big struggle, or we can sashay in and out of life's stages, grabbing on to each moment with glee. My dad still feels pretty good in his early 90s, and I feel terrific in my 60s. Sometimes I think I feel better than I did in my 30s, when I was up to my eyeballs raising four children. I'm experiencing more *thrills* than ever before, thanks to more exciting vacations; outdoor activities; and adventures with fun, energetic friends.

On a picnic years ago, I watched a woman step onto a boggy area, take a spill, and sink into muddy, sandy goo. *Spills* are for adults as well as children. When I was in my 40s, I went to a workshop and was asked to write something using my five senses. Life's *drills* are never over. And *bills?* We will always have those, but one way of looking at them is as evidence that we are living life to the fullest. I don't let them get me down anymore.

Ills and *pills?* They're all around us. Sickness and disease can happen at age 2, 22, or 102. If we eat right and exercise, we are doing our part. And *wills?* Mine's all set. Now I have time to focus on *thrills*— the stage I like the best.

Today I will not act my age, and I will get at least one thrill. Perhaps I will go ice-skating.

Strive for Greatness

*"I never wanted to be famous.
I only wanted to be great."*

Ray Charles

Scan the magazine covers as you wait in the checkout line, and you will see plenty of famous faces. But how many of them are also great? Some are, most definitely—the ones who work hard, practice, and make the most of their talent. The ones who are simply famous but have not worked hard and do not appear to have any real talent? They are not so great in the grand scheme of things, right? Credited as the Father of Soul and dubbed "The Genius" by Frank Sinatra, Ray Charles certainly realized his dream of becoming a great musician.

Today I will strive to be great, even if it is just in my small corner of the world. I will practice my talent or donate time and energy to a cause I believe in.

Daily Bits of Joy

*"Human felicity is produced not so much by
great pieces of good fortune that seldom happen,
as by little advantages that occur every day."*

Benjamin Franklin

Felicity is joy. Joy doesn't happen every day in
big, bowl-you-over ways, but we can savor
the small, beautiful moments: a child's smile as
he or she swings at the park; the look in your
elderly neighbor's eyes when you stop for a brief
chat instead of saying a hurried hello as you rush
right on by; catching up with a friend over dinner.
These are small moments, but taken together, they
contribute to a joyful existence.

**Each time I experience joy today, I will jot it down.
The moments will bring me joy all over again
when I review them tonight over a cup of hot tea.**

February 27

Out of Control

"The life of inner peace, being harmonious and without stress, is the easiest type of existence."

Norman Vincent Peale

Rush, rush, rush! Life's a maze, and the speed with which we must traverse the maze seems to get faster by the week. Studies reveal that when people are asked to define their past week in one word, the most common answers are *stressful* and *hectic*. It does not have to be this way.

This morning I will go over my plan for the day and cross one unnecessary task off my list. Perhaps I will do it tomorrow, next week, or next month. I have enough on my plate for today, and I want time to focus and savor each moment.

The Art of Healing

*"Healing is a matter of time, but it is
sometimes also a matter of opportunity."*

Hippocrates

*M*ost wounds will heal if we give them time.
Some ailments, however, are too big and
overwhelming to handle on our own. For these
ailments, we need to take the initiative and seek
healing. We need to find a professional to help us.

**Today I will reflect on the status of my life. If any
element is out of order—whether it is my finances;
my relationships; my state of mind; my diet;
my exercise routine; or perhaps even gambling,
alcohol, or other addictive issues—I will seek help.
I will seize the opportunity to heal.**

February 29

Tough Times, Easy Times

"In the depth of winter I finally learned that within me there lay an invincible summer."

Albert Camus

Just as cold, gray days help us appreciate warm, sunny days, the hard times we go through in life show us what we are made of, deep inside. What experiences have you gone through that helped you realize your strengths? For me, I never knew how strong and capable I was until I found myself alone with four children to feed. It was overwhelming at first, but I took it one day at a time—one small solution at a time—until I was amazed at my own ingenuity. What a glorious feeling—I felt like I could take on anything that life threw at me. It is when you despair of having nowhere to turn that you realize you can depend on yourself.

Today I will reflect on a time when I have been amazed at something I was able to do or conquer. I will think about my specific strengths, and I will make a point to use them.

My Time

"Dost thou love life? Then do not squander time; for that's the stuff life is made of."

Benjamin Franklin

*E*ach day includes twenty-four hours—eight for sleeping, eight for working, eight for everything else. Those last ones are the most important. The eight hours a day that we're not sleeping or working are the hours that define us. Are we wasting them all on reality TV, shopping for things we don't need, surfing the Internet, playing the same video or computer games over and over, sitting on the couch eating too much junk, yakking on the phone, texting ad infinitum, or bickering? Or are we doing interesting things, good-for-our-mind-or-body things, family things, and social things?

Today I will pay special attention to how I use "my" hours. I will endeavor to eat a healthy, leisurely meal with a family member or friend; take a long walk; and read, write, or watch something insightful.

March 2

Promises, Promises

"Better today than tomorrow morning."

Irish Proverb

/ like the fact that this quote comes from the Irish, who are known to end many days with laughter, argument, backslapping, and plenty of Irish whiskey or ale in a neighborhood pub. So, definitely—after a night like that—the morning after is not the best time to get anything done. The day before *is*... and then, of course, you really have something to celebrate with your friends at the pub. But let's also look at the word *procrastinate*. I like that partial word *cras* in the middle. *Crass* means crude and unrefined, lacking in sensibility. And when we procrastinate, we are certainly lacking in sensibility.

Today I will not procrastinate. I will do what needs to be done. I will wash those windows that have been waiting for my touch since last spring.

Young at Heart

"The heart that loves is always young."

Greek Proverb

Have you ever known someone for a while and had assumed they were in their 20s, but later found out they were actually nearing 40? Or has the opposite ever happened—you thought someone was in their late 40s, but later discovered they were only around 30? What is it—just good or bad genes? I honestly believe it is 90 percent attitude, just like the above quote implies. If you are happy and have a loving outlook, you can seem much younger than your years. But be careful! The reverse is also true. If you do not have a happy, loving outlook, you will likely appear (and feel) old before your time. Some studies have shown a negative outlook can actually subtract years from your life! Eat right, exercise, and love—those three things will keep you feeling like a 20-something well into your middle years.

Today I resolve to step out into the world with a loving outlook.

March 4

You're in There

"To dream of the person you would like to be is to waste the person you are."

Anonymous

*O*ur celebrity culture really messes us up. We find ourselves surrounded by photos of Jennifer Aniston, Angelina Jolie, Brad Pitt, Derek Jeter, Tom Brady, and Giselle. We read about their daily lives, their relationships, their goals, and dreams; we sit there, numb to our own relationships, goals, and dreams. We need to shake it off and get on with our own lives!

Today I am going to reflect upon my own talents, hopes, and dreams, and I'm going to get to work. Maybe I will take a class or apply for a job that will bring me one step closer to achieving a dream.

A Little Kindness

"One kind word can warm three winter months."

Japanese Proverb

In 1984, I was writing commercials for a radio station in Milwaukee. During the hectic, stressful weeks before the holidays, I was bombarded with requests from the sales department to write more and more ads for all the businesses that wanted to advertise during the holidays. One young woman, a sales department new-hire, took the time one day to write a note that she placed on my typewriter. "Pat, you are a gem and a treasure. Thank you for your hard work." Those few words filled my heart with enough oomph that I sailed through the busy holiday season that year. I tacked her note to my bulletin board and glanced at it often during the next year. It spurred me on to do an even better job for the salespeople.

Today I will write an "atta-girl" or "atta-boy" note to someone I work with. Then tonight I'll do the same for someone in my family.

Enemies or Allies?

"Without a hint of irony I can say I have been blessed with brilliant enemies....I owe them a great debt, because they redoubled my energies and drove me in new directions."
Edward O. Wilson

Can enemies really be a blessing? Talk about taking a fresh look at a situation! Think back over the enemies you've had in your life. The examples do not even have to be that dramatic—it could just be a neighbor or coworker you've never really hit it off with. Have they ever said something to you that maybe a friend never would—some criticism that hurt at first but made you work harder or changed your perspective? Fresh takes— even those that do not seem helpful or constructive at first—can lead us to new and better things.

Today if I have a run-in with anyone, I am going to try to see it as a possible opportunity for growth, rather than as a blow to my spirit. That person driving like a maniac on the expressway? They have come into my life to help me practice my patience.

Bravo! Well done!

*"A slowness to applaud betrays a cold
temper or an envious spirit."*

Hannah More

Think back to the last time something
wonderful happened to a friend or family
member. Was your first instinct to congratulate
them warmly, or did you feel a twinge of envy? The
first reaction is the healthier one, and the one we
would want our friends to have for us. Happiness
and good cheer are contagious; the next thing you
know, good fortune will come your way as well.
If you spend your life focusing on what you don't
have...well, there are always going to be things
we want that are out of our grasp, right? Focus on
what you do have, and your life will be truly good.

**If I feel envy creeping into my spirit today, I will
turn it into words of praise for the other person.
It may not feel genuine at first, but with practice,
I can change my attitude.**

Just Keep Going—
You'll Get There

"You must do the thing you think you cannot do."

Eleanor Roosevelt

After my first marriage fell apart, I never dreamed I could make it on my own with three small children to support. I can now look back and be proud of all I have accomplished, however. I am a stronger person because of the obstacles I have overcome. The trick is to not overthink it—otherwise it will be overwhelming. Just keep going, taking one small step at a time, and you will achieve your dreams.

Today I will face my fears. I will think about something I have always wanted to do but have been too afraid to go for. I will take one small step in the right direction. I will sign up for that business class—even though it involves making a presentation to the class at the end. I will know my stuff, and I will succeed.

Stimulating Conversation

"The need to be right all the time is the biggest bar to new ideas. It is better to have enough ideas for some of them to be wrong than to be always right by having no ideas at all."

Edward de Bono

My friends and I are all big talkers who love keeping up with current events. When we get together, the conversation is scintillating; often by the end of the night my opinion on a topic has turned completely around. This is one of my favorite things about my group of friends—we all respect and care about each other, so no one is afraid to give an opinion or enter into a discussion. We all bring something to the table, and we all learn from each other.

If an opportunity arises to discuss an important topic today, I will embrace it. I will not be afraid to express my opinion or listen to someone else's point of view.

Dream It, Then Do It

*"We know what we are,
but know not what we may be."*

William Shakespeare

Too often, when a dream or idea comes to mind, we push it away with thoughts such as these: *Don't try it—it's too hard. You're not smart enough. You don't have enough money.* These negative thoughts are the ones we should be pushing out of our minds! Start training yourself to think positive thoughts: *Why not me? How can I get started on this?*

I will begin working toward one dream today. Perhaps I will sign up for a baking or cooking class, and I will be on my way to my dream of opening my own bakery.

Embrace Hope

"Hope swells my sail."

James Montgomery

*M*ost of us love bright, brand-new days because of the hope that comes with them. We can take a deep breath, stretch, and start fresh. That fight we had with our spouse, our sibling, or our coworker? That belongs to yesterday. Today we embrace hope.

Today, no matter what I encounter, I will have hope. Even if things start to go wrong, my hopeful attitude will keep my mind and my being steady, and things will not go into a complete tailspin.

Thinkers v. Doers

*"Small deeds done are better than
great deeds planned."*

Peter Marshall

*A*re you a thinker or a doer? A dreamer or a
planner? A dreamer dreams of a trip
around the world in 80 days. A planner understands
that a 10-day trip to Europe is more realistic
and begins saving, mapping out the itinerary,
and packing the suitcase. Thinkers ponder great
problems, analyze many different ways to solve the
problems, write up big plans—but somehow never
get around to actually doing a blessed thing. Doers
chop a huge project into bite-size pieces, bite off
one piece, and get the job done. Small deeds done—
over and over—are what change the world.

**Today I will contact my favorite charity and
volunteer for one small project.**

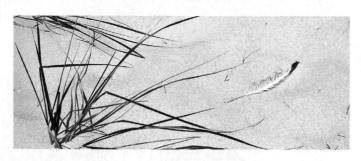

Shoulders Back, Head Up

"There ain't no man can avoid being born average.
But there ain't no man got to be common."

Satchel Paige

*L*et's face it: Probably 98 percent of the people in the world are average. Most of us aren't heads of state, brilliant scientists, CEOs, or supremely talented artists. We may be average, but we sure don't have to be common. *Common* expects too much without giving anything in return. *Common* is taking the lazy way out, and surely we can do better than that.

Today I will endeavor to stand out from the crowd in at least one small way. I will be upbeat even if I seem to have every reason to sulk.

The Whole Truth and Nothing But

"No man has a good enough memory to be a successful liar."

Abraham Lincoln

Lying often seems like the easier way out, but it usually ends up zapping our time and our energy. The one little lie that gets the ball rolling comes out so easily, but keeping up with all the little lies that breed from the one little lie—that's where it gets complicated. It isn't really worth it, is it? Plus, have you ever just blurted out the truth and later realized how refreshing it was, how real? It gave you the opportunity to have a real discussion and probably pushed a relationship to a deeper, truer level. Just discuss whatever happened—don't overcomplicate things.

Today I will be truthful.

Be Your Own Talk Meter

"Though there is no bone in the tongue,
it has frequently broken a man's head."

Irish Proverb

The ability to speak is among our greatest gifts. But this gift can also hurt or even destroy. Have you ever said something that you quickly regretted? Most of us have. Wouldn't it be nice if there were a talk meter that analyzed our words before anyone heard them? "No, you can't say that to your 5-year-old daughter—your opinion means the world to her. Revise that a little so you can help her learn without shattering her spirit." Yes, a talk meter would be nice.

Today, I will think before I talk. If I get angry, I will take deep breaths and choose my words carefully.

March 16

Create a Home for the Beautiful

"Though we travel the world over to find the beautiful, we must carry it with us or we find it not."

Ralph Waldo Emerson

Call to mind the most beautiful things you've ever seen: Ireland's rolling green hills; the sunrise over the Grand Canyon; the horizon across an endless lake; perfect blue hydrangeas in the thick of summer; Chagall's magnificent paintings; a majestic dolphin swimming and jumping among the rolling waves. If we take true notice of beautiful things, they reach into our being and become an integral part of a magnificent life. We can call them to mind and perhaps visit them again, or they can lead us on to ever more beautiful experiences.

I will be on the lookout for the beautiful throughout this day.

Laugh 'Til It Hurts

"Humor is not a trick, not jokes. Humor is a presence in the world—like grace—and shines on everybody."

Garrison Keillor

Humor and the laughter that accompanies it is a sweet, delicate thing. Sometimes it's just a chuckle. Sometimes it begins deep in the gut and erupts, leaving us heaving for air. You can almost see Uncle Bob doubling over from fits of laughter even though you're in the other room. Humor is contagious, and it adds spice to our lives.

Today I will tell a funny story to a lonely neighbor. I will do my part to spread the joy.

Let Go

*"Everything comes gradually and
at its appointed hour."*

Ovid

Have you ever wanted something so badly and only received it after you stopped looking for it? After you were done with school, did you submit what seemed like a million job applications? Then you kept your phone on you at all times, checking it every five minutes. Then weeks later—out of nowhere—that great opportunity came along. Or what about when you were feeling lonely and yearning for companionship? At that time you probably were not exuding happiness or seeming particularly fun to be around, but once you "gave up," you met the love of your life in the most unlikely of places. It's funny how that happens— once we let go, wonderful opportunities arise.

Today I will be patient. I will enjoy the present and not try to make anything happen before its time.

Seize the Moment

*"Between saying and doing many a
pair of shoes is worn out."*

Italian Proverb

*M*any of us are born procrastinators. If you're like me, you can think up hundreds of ways and thousands of excuses to put off doing something you may not enjoy doing but that must be done, nonetheless. Between here and finally filing all the papers stacked in a dozen piles on my dining room table, I will make a thousand trips around my condo and around town. *I'd rather vacuum than sort those papers. I'll wash dishes before I'll organize that mess.* I'm wearing out another pair of shoes as I systematically avoid what would probably take me only an hour to finish.

Oh, all right. Today I will organize so I can actually serve my friends an amazing dinner on my beautiful dining room table.

A True Friend

*"My best friend is the one who
brings out the best in me."*

Henry Ford

My best friend constantly sings my praises
to others. When it's just the two of us,
though, she does not hesitate to call me out when
she disagrees with something I've said or done.
That time I spent days cooped up inside with
the exception of work because a breakup left me
devastated? She is the one who dragged me out
to a funny movie and then for a cup of tea so we
could have a heart to heart. When I was hesitant
about going after my dream because of "practical
concerns," she pointed out that I would likely regret
not taking the opportunity that was in front of me.

**Today I will send my friend a note. I will sing her
praises and thank her for all she has done for me.**

Character Is Priceless

"Character is better than wealth."

Irish Proverb

*W*ealth can be achieved in many different ways. It can be earned through years of long, hard work, but it can also be the result of an inheritance or winning the lottery. Character is priceless, isn't it? It is something you cultivate all the years of your life. Every experience, every choice, every mistake—all the work you do cultivates your unique character. It is the prize for a lifetime of work and struggle. Plus, it is completely your own masterpiece. You cannot inherit or purchase character.

Today I will try to add to my character by volunteering at my neighborhood community center. Perhaps I can tutor a struggling student.

March 22

The Joy of Springtime

*"If we had no winter, the spring
would not be so pleasant."*

Anne Bradstreet

Spring tends to take us by surprise each year,
doesn't it? In the dead of winter, it is hard
to fathom that it will ever be spring or summer
again. But before we know it, we hear those first
chirps. What a glorious feeling! It is a lot like our
lives, isn't it? We would not appreciate the glorious
vacations as much if we didn't have the typical,
ho-hum workdays. And we would not appreciate the
weddings and other joyous events so much if we
did not also have the funerals and other sorrowful
times. What amazing lives we lead.

**Today I will not only appreciate this fine spring day
by taking a walk in the neighborhood—I will also
be mindful that without struggles in life, I would
not appreciate the joyous occasions so much.**

Here Comes the Sun

*"Experience is what you get while
looking for something else."*
Federico Fellini

You go visit your grandmother, but what do you get in addition? A trip to the art museum to see a fascinating art glass exhibit; dinner at a German restaurant, where Grandma orders in her native tongue; a lesson in how to make the perfect piecrust; the opportunity to see Grandma's wrinkled hands up close when you help her with her manicure; a chance to learn canasta when Grandma's girlfriends come over for a visit. Life happens and horizons expand on the way to our destinations.

I will go about my plan for today, but I will also be aware that everything that happens will add to the store of experience that makes my life unique.

Introducing: The Real Me

"One of the greatest moments in anybody's developing experience is when he no longer tries to hide from himself but determines to get acquainted with himself as he really is."

Norman Vincent Peale

You see them from time to time: wordless, eyes shifting downward, legs registering just enough energy to shuffle along. These are the shy ones—people whose lives have left them bruised, scared, and lonely. Hiding from life keeps them feeling safe and cozy. I say, "Stand tall!" When you step out of your fear and into a tiny bit of the limelight, rainbows happen. What are you afraid of? That you don't measure up to everyone else? We are all good—just different, which actually makes each of us that much more special.

Today I will reflect on my interests, and I will join a club. Maybe I will make a new friend.

A Joyful Outlook

"'On with the dance, let the joy be unconfined!'
is my motto, whether there's any dance
to dance or any joy to unconfine."

Mark Twain

One of my favorite things to do is speak to audiences about *Humor for the Health of It.* I use a suitcase full of props, including my rubber chicken collection, to demonstrate just how easy it is to put more laughter in our lives. At one point I tell the audience to laugh. They look at me dumbfounded because I haven't said anything funny. Then a few snickers begin, and soon the whole room is belly laughing. Humor puts people at ease and brings us together; a bitter, cynical, negative attitude just pushes people farther away.

Today I will keep smiling, no matter what. A positive outlook is good for my health and well-being, and you never know when something wonderful is just around the corner.

Brain Strain

"Intelligence without ambition is a bird without wings."
Salvador Dalí

*I*f you find that you have a gift or talent, you should share it, right? Wouldn't it be a shame if someone with an amazing voice just sang in their own room all day? Whatever talent we have, we should put it to use in the world around us.

Today I will reflect on my talents, and I will put at least one of them to use. Maybe I will draft an article about a topic of interest to me and submit it to a newspaper, magazine, or Web site.

Focus on the Here and Now

*"True generosity toward the future consists
in giving everything to the present."*
Albert Camus

When you look at the world around you, what needs fixing? Is our government overspending, pushing our children and grandchildren deeper into debt? Research candidates for political office, and make sure they are using tax revenue as efficiently as possible. Are our parks and cultural institutions being kept up? Volunteer at one of them. Pick up trash at the park or join a committee at the local museum or nature center. Did you know that the average American will have created 52 tons of garbage by age 75 and that each of us goes through nearly 5,000 gallons of fresh water a month? Yikes! Make changes now, and it will improve life for present generations and future ones.

Today I will make a positive change to help my current world and the world of the future. When I go to the grocery store, I will buy a few reusable bags to hold my groceries. I will keep them in my trunk so I can use them on the next trip as well. Good-bye, flimsy plastic grocery bags!

March 28

An Organized, Breathable Space

"Out of clutter, find simplicity. From discord, find harmony. In the middle of difficulty lies opportunity."
Albert Einstein

On a scale of one to ten, I'm a seven and my sister is a ten when it comes to maintaining order in our lives. After her latest move, she got rid of everything she didn't need and set up a brilliant organization system. I, on the other hand, have lived in my place for years and am still trying to figure out how to organize all my stuff. I keep way too many things that I don't use, and "organized clutter" doesn't bother me like it should. I know my sister's style is much better.

Today I will do one job well. I will organize the closet I have taken to calling my "auxiliary kitchen."

Life Improves with Age

"I feel like an ostrich who has finally pulled its
head out of the sand and loves what it sees....
I love getting older, things get easier every day."

Jane Powell

When I hit 30, I didn't like it. I had three kids under four years of age, I never had a moment to myself, and I was on the verge of divorce. In my 40s I was in a new, healthy relationship; I made just enough money to pay my bills; and I began to travel the world. My 50s were also great—more traveling and more freedom in my career. Then came 60—the best ever. I'd just moved to Florida, where my frozen Wisconsin bones could finally thaw out, and I had found my soul mate. I've learned that getting older means getting to do exactly what I want, when I want to do it. Life for seniors nowadays is positively delicious; I wouldn't want to go back and start over for anything.

I will make the most of today. I will bike my usual ten miles, then wander over to the art museum. Maybe I will talk one of my friends into taking a painting class or planning a trip with me.

Love Involves Hard, Wonderful Work

"Life is to be fortified by many friendships.
To love and to be loved
is the greatest happiness of existence."

Aesop

*N*otice that this quote does not simply state, "To be loved is the greatest happiness of existence." Merely being loved without feeling loving in return does not bring us the true happiness we so desire.

It takes work to love someone—lots of work. Whether we are talking about loving a parent, a child, or a soul mate, loving is hard work. You must remember their birthdays and other special occasions. You must listen when they are hurt or sad and think of unique, crafty ways to take their minds off their troubles. You must be there for them when they are sick or in need in some other way. At times you must even put a loved one's needs ahead of your own. Yes, loving is hard work, but oh, what gratifying, wonderful work.

Most of us are lucky enough to have many loved ones, so it is all one big exchange. Last year—as I was busy lovingly helping my elderly parents—my loving children were planning a wonderful surprise party for my upcoming birthday. While I was doing the work of love, I was receiving love in return many times over. Love is certainly one glorious concept.

Today I will act lovingly toward someone close to me, and I will tuck their smiles into my heart.

Letting Go of Anger

"Let your anger set with the sun
and not rise again with it."

Irish Proverb

*H*ow many times have you heard the advice to never go to bed angry? It seems simple enough, but when the situation arises, it is so tempting to be stubborn and wait for your loved one to take the first step. But if you both remain stubborn, your dispute will carry over into the next day—perhaps into the next week, the next month, and the next year. Be the proactive one—talk the problem out with your loved one. Any problem can be resolved if you both try. One will likely have to apologize, and the other will likely have to forgive. Or perhaps you both have some apologizing and forgiving to do. Just get the discussion started—you will sleep better, and tomorrow truly will be a fresh, new day.

If I become upset with anyone close to me today, I will sit down and chat with them before the sun sets.

Don't Play the Fool

"If 50 million people say a foolish thing, it is still a foolish thing."

Anatole France

Have you ever gone along with an idea even though you had an inkling it wasn't right? Then later, when it proved to be wrong, you said to yourself, *I knew it all along!* We need to trust our instincts sooner rather than later. Hindsight is 20/20, but we need to have the confidence to separate from the group early in the process.

Today I will make my own decisions. I may end up going along with a group idea, but only if I feel certain it is the right path to take.

April 2

One Little Step After Another

"Perseverance will accomplish all things."
American Proverb

*M*ost things we desire take perseverance, don't they? When groups of citizens in a young country banded together to resist laws they believed were unfair, they persevered and won their freedom. Years later different groups of people banded together to end slavery, and again, freedom was gained through perseverance. What if those people had not persevered? It would have been easy to just quit, but we are thankful for their perseverance.

Today, if a job or task tires or deflates me, I will not give in until it is finished. I will persevere, and my perseverance will make me proud.

Unzipping My Soul

"Don't be so humble—you are not that great."

Golda Meir

As a professional speaker, I know that we love listening to our own introductions. The MC generally blathers on and on about our accomplishments. By the time it is my turn to speak, I am usually embarrassed enough that I begin by telling the audience, "I've been married, divorced, and annulled twice. My second husband left me for an older woman. I raised four kids as a single parent, had them in college for 17 years in a row, and never earned more than $27,000 a year in my life." With that the audience relaxes, knowing I'm one of them. I don't act humble, just real.

Today I resolve to be real—not snobby, but not overly humble either.

April 4

Beating the Odds

"For every failure, there's an alternative course of action. You just have to find it. When you come to a roadblock, take a detour."

Mary Kay Ash

It takes guts to continue when nothing seems to be going your way. Think of the Wright brothers in their struggle to invent a flying machine. They worked for thousands of hours on some designs, but many of their test flights lasted only a few seconds. The first flight, by Orville, was only 120 feet long and took 12 seconds. Today a sign hanging in the Smithsonian reads, "As inventors, builders, and flyers they further developed the aeroplane, taught man to fly, and opened the era of aviation." Wow—it was all certainly worth it, wasn't it?

If I face failure today, I will not despair. I will try again.

Hitting Another Single

"Give what you have. To some it may be better than you dare think."

Henry Wadsworth Longfellow

We all have unique gifts and talents—we don't have to be the player with the strength to hit the ball out of the park. More than 5,000 home runs were hit during the 2009 major-league baseball season. Seems like a lot, doesn't it? But that same year, nearly 34,000 singles were hit. Seven times more singles than home runs. More games are won by singles than homers. Do what you do best. It is enough, and it amazes more people than you realize.

Today I will go about my work with a smile. I will give it my all, and if somebody happens to notice my effort, it'll be that much more rewarding.

The Good Ol' Days

*"I have learned that success is to be measured
not so much by the position that one has
reached in life as by the obstacles
which he has overcome while trying to succeed."*

Booker T. Washington

The struggles we face on our life journeys give us that fine patina that we can eventually claim as wisdom. Having been blessed with a carefree childhood, it never occurred to me that I might end up struggling financially to raise four children on my own. Once it was my reality, however, I embraced it and grew from the struggles that came along with it. With those struggles came confidence and greater empathy for others.

Today I will face each struggle with confidence and determination.

The Sweet Scent of Forgiveness

*"Forgiveness is the fragrance the violet
sheds on the heel that has crushed it."*

Mark Twain

It's hard—very hard—to forgive someone who has
violated your trust or crushed your spirit. But
human beings actually have an amazing capacity
for forgiveness. I will never forget the episode of
The Oprah Winfrey Show in which a mother forgave
the man who murdered her child. *How did she do
it,* I wondered. *Her heart must be the size of several
football fields.* But then I realized it is the most
beautiful way to make peace with something that
cannot be undone. It does not erase the wrong,
but it succeeds in casting a veil of beauty over it.
Rather than lashing out and living with bitterness,
the mother preserved her own dignity and that of
her lost loved one.

**Today if someone hurts me, I will forgive and
preserve the beautiful.**

April 8

Recharge Your Batteries

"It is a common experience that a problem difficult at night is resolved in the morning after the committee of sleep has worked on it."

John Steinbeck

We all need to recharge, don't we? Only sometimes we don't realize it, and we grow more and more frustrated as we try harder and harder but get nowhere. Then we walk away and a short time later, voilà—the solution we were looking for. Our minds just needed that break.

If I find myself frustrated while working on a difficult problem today, I will take a break— perhaps even until tomorrow morning.

Appreciating the Weeds

"A good garden may have some weeds."

Thomas Fuller

One small weed does not ruin a lovely garden, does it? If the gardener allows the weed to multiply and take over the garden, yes, the garden will be ruined. A weed here and there is natural, however. Just like with us, right? We will never be perfect, but we are still good overall. Take notice of any imperfections and work on them, but do not despair.

Today I will reflect on myself. I will be honest about my flaws and work on them, but I will not get discouraged.

Becoming Whole

"Life is a series of experiences, each one of which makes us bigger, even though sometimes it is hard to realize."

Henry Ford

We each face a different set of experiences, and this is what makes our life uniquely ours. This is an amazing thing to ponder—all the different experiences, all the different lives. Each experience we face makes us stronger and more prepared for the next experience. This is true even when at first an experience appears to be a negative one, whether it is a relatively small negative experience (such as the frustration of getting lost) or a large negative experience (such as the death of a loved one). We face each experience with the strength and wisdom we have achieved through past experiences. Each experience moves us forward and fills out the little spaces in our psyches that need to be filled out. And finally—we are who we were meant to be.

Today I will not shrink from any experience; I know I can handle anything that comes my way because I have the wisdom from all my past experiences.

When Tragedy Strikes

"Courage is grace under pressure."

Ernest Hemingway

How do you react in a time of emergency? Do you keep your head, or do you completely lose it? Once, when I was spending time with some family members at my condo, one of them was looking out the window and spotted a woman lying on her back in the middle of the parking lot below. One of us called 9-1-1, and two of us raced down the stairs. Once we made it over to the woman, we cradled her head, and she came to. We kept her still, comforted her, and made sure she didn't move. We were relieved when the EMTs arrived and took over, but we felt good about the fact that we acted courageously, even though we were scared half to death.

Today if a serious problem arises, I will step forward to help instead of shrinking into the background.

April 12

All Aboard!

*"Logic will get you from A to B.
Imagination will take you everywhere."*

Albert Einstein

Getting from A to B can be boring and routine, or it can be magical and memorable. Take a cross-country trip to see Grandma, for instance. Wouldn't you rather be in the car that takes some detours and sees some sights along the way? Sure, there will be trips that have to be more rushed and time won't allow for it, but where possible, it's healthy and fun to stretch our minds while we stretch our legs.

Today I will do at least one thing that strays from my usual routine. Perhaps I will get up a little earlier and take a walk or jog before work.

Best Foot Forward

"We shouldn't want to look like anybody but ourselves, because we are the people we were intended to be."

Dixie Carter

I've got age spots, gray hair that I color blonde, and wrinkles around my eyes. I've earned each and every aspect of my growing-older face. I like my face. It's the only one I'll ever have. I am not going to lift it, stretch it, or make anything smaller or bigger. I just want to be me—nobody else. I'm not aiming for perfection, and in fact, the older I get, the less makeup I wear. I now know that a smile is the best makeup ever invented.

Today I will identify one aspect of my looks that I love and that sets me apart from everyone else in the world.

Say "Aaaaahhhhhh"

"We are continually faced by great opportunities brilliantly disguised as insolvable problems."

Benjamin Franklin

When I hear the phrase "insolvable problem" these days, health care is the first thing that comes to mind. It is such a huge issue, but we have conquered bigger problems in the past, haven't we? I know if we all come together, we can come up with a better system, and future generations will marvel at our ingenuity.

Today I will do my part to address the health care crisis facing my community. I will either volunteer at a nursing home in my neighborhood, or I will get on board and help elect a candidate I trust with this issue.

Shake Things Up

"As long as you live, keep learning how to live."

Seneca

We live our lives a little differently with each passing year, don't we? Often the changes are subtle, so we may not notice the impact they have on our lives. Change is invigorating and inspiring, and each new experience opens more doors.

Today I will shake up my routine in some way. Perhaps I'll try out a new recipe or give my car a break and ride my bike to work.

How to Be Memorable

*"The key to immortality is first living
a life worth remembering."*

Augustine of Hippo

Think of all the memorable people throughout history—George Washington, Susan B. Anthony, Vincent van Gogh, Martin Luther King Jr. They all worked toward different goals, but they were all dedicated to those goals and worked hard to achieve them. Think of the memorable people in your own family and community as well. The ones we most admire were the ones who, over the course of their entire life, left a legacy of dedication to high ideals. If we emulate these virtues in our own lives, we will be remembered as well.

Today I will work hard and do my best on each task I face. If an opportunity arises, I will step forward and help someone else, as well.

Making Our Own "Happily Ever After"

"To live happily is an inward power of the soul."

Marcus Aurelius

Our lives are not perfect. We need to be mindful of the elements that *are* working, though, and then work on the rest, bit by bit. What makes you happy every day? Maybe you are thankful that you have a wonderful family, or great friends, or the best dog in the world, or a challenging job that offers interesting opportunities. On the other hand, what are the things you would change if you could? Do you wish you were more fit? Start going for a walk each morning or afternoon. Are you unhappy with your job? Think about what you love to do, and take a class or join a group that will help you get closer to doing what you want to do. Be thankful for the good things in your life, and make progress on the rest. That's all you have to do.

Today I will be thankful for at least one thing that makes me happy, and I will make progress toward achieving a dream.

April 18

Communication by Silence

"Well-timed silence hath more eloquence than speech."

Martin Fraquhar Tupper

Years ago—when I was struggling with what to say to a friend who had just been diagnosed with cancer—I was particularly attentive to the sermon at church one Sunday. Pastor Bill was focusing on "communication by silence."

Pastor Bill explained that he'd visited a member of the parish in the hospital. The man was recovering from serious surgery, and it was very difficult for him to talk. After a few initial questions about how the man was feeling, Bill launched into talking about the weather. Then Bill realized that the man probably had little interest in what the weather was like outside. So Bill leaned back in his chair and just sat.

Every few minutes, Pastor Bill looked at the man and smiled. Once in a while, he'd pat the man's hand. He sat with the man for more than an hour. During that time, it occurred to Bill that he and the man were very in tune with each other, even though they were not speaking. The man seemed relieved that he didn't have to make small talk and

116

appeared comforted by Pastor Bill's presence. Pastor Bill thought about how brave the man was to endure the pain of his condition. He thought about how he too, would like it if someone came and just sat with him if he were ever in the hospital and really didn't feel up to talking. Just to have someone there—especially someone not assigned to be there to take care of him physically, but there just to be a comforting presence.

That sermon was life-altering for me. I learned that the close proximity of another human being is often what makes the difference in how we react to pain, fear, and loneliness. Even couples don't have to be talking all the time. My dear friend Jack and I can sit in the same room, reading, neither of us speaking. Every so often we sneak quick glances at each other, but it is so peaceful and refreshing to just have that quiet time together.

I will try to be a comforting presence to someone in need today.

Never Give Up

"Many of life's failures are people who did not realize how close they were to success when they gave up."

Thomas Alva Edison

One of Albert Einstein's teachers described him as "mentally slow, unsociable, and adrift forever in foolish dreams." Good thing Einstein didn't take those criticisms to heart, right? Henry Ford went broke five different times before he succeeded. Michael Jordan was cut from his high school basketball team. Success comes through perseverance and hard work.

If I get discouraged today, I will take a break—and then get back to work. I will not give up.

Rock Your World

*"No one can make you feel inferior
without your consent."*

Eleanor Roosevelt

We really are all equal, aren't we? We are not the same—we all have our own unique talents—but we are all equal. The eloquent senator may have a firm grasp on the politics of trade in the global economy, but when his car breaks down at the worst moment, he is in awe of the skills of the mechanic down the street. We all have different strengths and are good at different things. An inferiority complex is just a state of mind; it can be a cop-out, even, because it's an excuse not to try. Keep your head up, shoulders back, and get to work.

Today I will rock the world in my own special way. I will not feel inferior to anyone.

The Cycle of Life

"It takes a long time to become young."

Pablo Picasso

As twenty-somethings, we think we know everything, don't we? Then soon we get some experience under our belts, and we realize how little we know. Once we near 60, we have experienced a lot, and this makes us feel invincible and—you guessed it—young again. I am in my 60s, and I feel younger than ever. The kids are grown, and I have been through numerous and varied experiences. I can do all the things I only dreamed about during my younger years. It takes a lifetime to begin to live with the awe of a toddler, discovering the world one blade of grass at a time.

Today I will plan an excursion that will expand my mind and my horizons.

Kindness Is Strength

"When I was young, I used to admire intelligent people; as I grow older, I admire kind people."

Abraham Joshua Heschel

When we are young, it is easy to be amazed by how much older people know. As we grow older, though, we come to realize that knowing a lot comes from study, experience, and years. Kindness is harder to come by. It takes determination to remain kind. To be kind after being forced to wait in a long line because of a systems problem takes a great deal of understanding and self-control. To remain kind and loving at your core even when your heart has been broken over and over again seems to border on stupidity, doesn't it? But it isn't stupid—it is strong, hopeful, constructive, and beautiful.

Today I resolve to be kind, even if I begin to feel overwhelmed.

Less Is More

"Perfection is achieved, not when there is nothing more to add, but when there is nothing left to take away."

Antoine de Saint-Exupéry

As I learned to write, I was always instructed to reduce my written words to the bare minimum. Why repeat something that's already been said, even if you are using different words? In Stephen King's book *On Writing*, he states that the second draft equals the first draft, minus ten percent. Less is perfection.

Today—instead of blathering on and on about something—I will be brief, and I will be gone.

Follow Your Heart

"If you let people follow their feelings, they will be able to do good. This is what is meant by saying that human nature is good."

Mencius

I will never understand parents who try to persuade their child to follow a career that is more to the parents' liking than the child's. When one makes a career out of a dream or passion that's been nestled in one's heart, it's easy to look forward to going to work. Feeling fulfilled by our work fosters a more positive worldview, which helps us naturally focus on the good all around us.

Today if I feel the urge to do something different— whether it's to explore a neighborhood park or museum, take a class, see a particular movie, or try a new kind of food—I will go for it.

April 25

Try, Try Again

*"Anyone who has never made a mistake
has never tried anything new."*

Albert Einstein

Most of us could make a long list of things we've tried that didn't quite work out. I've made mistakes as a child, a student, a wife, a parent, a friend, and a soul mate. But I'm happy to report that every one of those mistakes taught me something that helped me to do better on a later endeavor.

Today I will not be afraid to try something new. If I fall down, I will have a good laugh and get right back up.

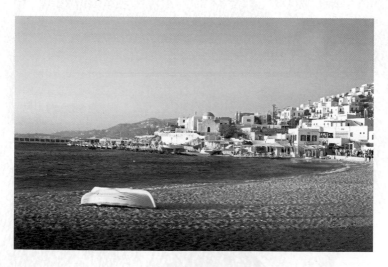

Go-for-It Greatness

"A pessimist is one who makes difficulties of his opportunities and an optimist is one who makes opportunities of his difficulties."

Harry S. Truman

When was the last time you got discouraged? Think of all the great people in history. There were probably times when they could have given up, right? Frederick Douglass could have just lived a quiet life as a free person rather than travel the country speaking out against slavery. But he likely noticed that people tended to listen when he talked; he probably felt a duty to keep speaking and fighting. It was not easy, but he believed in his country and the ideals it was founded upon. He knew things could be different, and he worked to change his country. That's optimism for you.

Today I will see each difficulty as an opportunity to learn and grow.

April 27

How Do You Do?

"You cannot shake hands with a clenched fist."

Indira Gandhi

The first step in forming a relationship with someone is openness, isn't it? Just like your heart and your head, your hand must be open, palm touching the palm of the person whose hand you're shaking. It's a sign of a willingness to be vulnerable. It's a simple thing, a handshake—given in peace and accepted with anticipation.

Today I will be open to all I encounter.

Always on the Lookout

"The intelligent man is always open to new ideas. In fact, he looks for them."

Proverbs 18:15 TLB

*N*ew ideas are energizing, aren't they? Doing the same thing the same way all the time can be comforting, but it does not energize us. New ideas give us that "Aha!" moment that is so invigorating. If something works, don't fix it, but don't close yourself off either. New ideas lead to growth, and growth is always a positive thing—for an individual and for a community.

If I find myself dreading a certain task at work (or even just around my house) today, I will try to think of a new way of seeing or doing it.

Rounding Home

"In the book of life, the answers aren't in the back."
Charles Schulz

We find ourselves on our own a lot in life. That can be scary, but it also can be beautiful. I choose to see it as beautiful. I run through life—arms flailing, laughing, kicking up my heels, skidding into the answers as they hit me smack in the face. Sure, I make mistakes—but I learn from them, and my performance on the next task is all the better for it. Bring it on.

I will embrace today—and all the mistakes and triumphs that come with it.

A Friend in Need

*"A friend is someone who is there for you
when he'd rather be anywhere else."*

Len Wein

Imagine it is a Friday night; it was a long week at work, and you are about to crawl into bed for a long night's sleep. Your phone rings—it is your dearest friend, and she has fallen and injured her ankle. She asks if you will take her to the emergency room. What do you do? You help her, even though the ER on a Friday night is the last place you would choose to be. You go because you are a good friend, and you know she'd do the same thing for you in a heartbeat.

Today I will go out of my way to be a good friend.

May 1

Dream Work

"You can't wait for inspiration.
You have to go after it with a club."

Jack London

Very few things just appear before us. Writers often discuss being frustrated by writer's block, but the basic truth is that inspiration is something that we must actively seek. If we just sit back and wait to be inspired, we will likely fall asleep on the couch before anything earth-shattering occurs to us. We have to get out there and do lots of different things. That's when great ideas come to us—not when we're just sitting around, doing nothing.

I will seek inspiration today, and it will come to me.

Our Tiny Corner of the World

"Do what you can, with what you have, where you are."

Theodore Roosevelt

*L*ife can be overwhelming. We see problems all around us, and it's easy to just throw up our hands. We need to stop feeling responsible for changing the world. We are only responsible for our tiny corner of it. If everyone took care of their tiny corner, *that* would change the world.

Today I will analyze my specific environment—my city or town, or even just my block. I will think about what needs to be done, and I will do one small thing to get the ball rolling.

The Extra Mile

"If a man is called to be a street sweeper,
he should sweep streets even as Michelangelo painted,
or Beethoven composed music, or Shakespeare
wrote poetry. He should sweep streets so well that
all the hosts of heaven and earth will pause to say:
Here lived a great street sweeper who did his job well."

Martin Luther King Jr.

After serving as a fighter pilot during World War II, my dad worked as a rural mail carrier in our small hometown. For 32 years he traversed 50 miles of country roads delivering mail to 500 patrons. He carried out his duties faithfully and went above and beyond when he felt a situation warranted it. When a letter arrived from a son or daughter serving overseas, he would walk up a long country lane in a foot of snow to save an anxious elderly couple the walk. We are not all called to be heads of state, but we are all asked to perform our jobs to the best of our abilities.

Today I will pay attention to even the smallest aspects of my job, and I will do my best.

Never Give Up

"Great works are performed not by strength, but perseverance."

Samuel Johnson

reat works do indeed take strength, but perseverance is the more important component. One burst of strength cannot accomplish the whole task, but continued strength over the long haul can get it done. Canals, railroads, expressways, the Sistine Chapel and other great works of art—none of these were accomplished in the space of a couple hours. We must keep at our work until our dreams are realized.

Today I will keep at my work, even if I begin to feel discouraged.

A Treasure Trove

"I would be the most content if my children grew up to be the kind of people who think decorating consists mostly of building enough bookshelves."

Anna Quindlen

*B*ooks really can take us anywhere. We read *Like Water for Chocolate*, for instance, and we feel like we are in Mexico. We learn about the culture, and it makes us want to taste some of the food we read about, or perhaps even travel to that country. Knowledge surely is the most important treasure to add to our lives.

Today I will go to my neighborhood library or bookstore. I will wander until I stumble upon something that captures my interest.

Cause a Stir

*"Would the world ever have been made
if its maker had been afraid of making trouble?
Making life means making trouble."*

George Bernard Shaw

What is trouble? Ask 20 people, and you will likely get 20 different answers—many of which will contradict each other. It is impossible to go through life without stirring up some kind of trouble. All we *can* do is go about our lives and our work; if we offend or "trouble" another, we must reflect upon whether or not we are in the wrong. If we are, we make amends. If we feel we are not in the wrong, we explain our side, and then move on. George Bernard Shaw never hesitated to say anything to anybody. Many people liked him, but a lot of other people did not. Such is life. We are not going to hit it off with everybody.

Today I will go about my life. If I get into any trouble, I will discuss it or make amends, and I will move on.

May 7

Becoming New Again

"One changes from day to day... every few years one becomes a new being."

George Sand

Research indicates that most cell and tissue types in the human body are much younger than the person in which they are found. Few cells live for the entire life of the person. As our bodies change, so too do our personalities, desires, and beliefs. I know I'm not the same loopy, lost-in-the-maze-of-the-world person I was in college. I'm not even the same will-I-ever-get-it-all-done frazzled mom I was in my 30s and 40s. I am new and improved.

Today I will ask a friend to join me in a celebratory lunch. What are we celebrating? The new me and the new her.

Care to Share?

*"A mother is a person who, seeing there are
only four pieces of pie for five people,
promptly announces she never did care for pie."*

Tenneva Jordan

We've all done it, and not just mothers either.
We sacrifice, share, and take care of others.
We really want the last piece of pie, but we also
know someone else probably wants it too. And so
we give it away. And in doing so, we grow. Most
of us learned this behavior at home, because we
caught on that it was done for us when we were
small or in need. Sharing and sacrifice is what
family is all about, and these components hold our
society together as well.

Today I will share in some small but beautiful way.

Now We're Cookin'

*"It is better to fail in originality
than to succeed in imitation."*

Herman Melville

It is tempting to imitate, isn't it? It is easy. But if we lead our lives in imitation of others, we are not being true to our own destiny. We need to heed those urges to try something new or take a different path.

Today I will listen to my inner voice.

Be a Dreamer *and* a Doer

*"The future belongs to those who believe
in the beauty of their dreams."*

Eleanor Roosevelt

Who built the marvelous world of today, with its machines and amazing capabilities? The people who just took life as it came to them with no thought to dreams or goals? No, for the most part, it was built by the people who noticed problems, came up with solutions, and worked until their goals were realized. It will be the same with the future—it will be formed by dreamers at work.

Today I will work toward a dream. Perhaps I will sign up for a class or attend a conference.

Just Take It All In

"The only means of strengthening one's intellect is to make up one's mind about nothing—to let the mind be a thoroughfare for all thoughts."

John Keats

From time to time, it is good for us to just explore, isn't it? Not to analyze every little thing, just wander and take it all in. It is the same with our brains. If we feed our brains the same general information all the time, they will grow lazy. We exercise our brains by picking up books on topics that are completely new to us. We don't have to form an opinion on it right away—it is actually better if we just take it in with no preconceived ideas. Analysis is for later, when we know more about the topic.

Today when I come across a word or topic I am unsure of, I will research it and take it all in. My brain feels energized already!

Follow the Muse

"Those who dare to fail miserably can achieve greatly."
Robert F. Kennedy

Greatness takes daring. Take Thomas Edison, Henry Ford, the Wright brothers, and Martin Luther King Jr. Many of the people of their eras probably thought they were crazy, dedicating all their time and efforts toward things that existed only in their dreams. But today we know better— we know they were brilliant.

Today I will be daring.

May 13

A Work of Art

"The world is but a canvas to our imaginations."
Henry David Thoreau

The world is our canvas, and my small part of the world is my canvas. Put all of our ideas and projects together, and it is an amazing masterpiece.

Today I will plant something beautiful, and I will nourish it. Flowers will be my contribution to our canvas.

Bigger, Better, Longer, Faster

"Do not follow where the path may lead…
Go instead where there is no path and leave a trail."

Ralph Waldo Emerson

*I*t can be tempting and comfortable to just follow in the footsteps of those who've gone before us. If everyone did that, though, where would change, growth, and innovation come from? It is better and healthier to try out new ideas now and then.

Today if a new idea or way of doing something occurs to me, I will give it a shot.

May 15

The Big Vote

"He who would leap high must take a long run."
Danish Proverb

*A*iming for anything worthwhile takes preparation, planning, stamina, and persistence. Take the child whose dream is to be an Olympian one day. This is not a simple dream to achieve, but if an individual is blessed with the right dose of talent, he or she can get there through focused training.

Today I will not give in to discouragement on my way to achieving my dream.

The Excitement of Life

"Every great and commanding moment in the annals of the world is the triumph of some enthusiasm."

Ralph Waldo Emerson

Think of some of the great moments in history: the American Revolution, the abolishment of slavery, the Berlin Wall coming down, the overthrow of apartheid. None of these things would have come about if people didn't have high ideals and fight for them.

Today I am going to take some time to reflect on the issues of the day. I will choose one that I am enthusiastic about, and I will join a group and start working toward progress.

The Royal Flush

*"Life consists not in holding good cards
but in playing those you hold well."*

Josh Billings

Some of us are born into wealth, some into
poverty. Some of us are born with amazing
talents or intellect; others of us have average
talents or intellect. The trick is to take inventory of
what we have, and then make the most of it. Who's
to say where our abilities and intellect can take us?

**Today I will make the most of the hand I've been
dealt. I will work hard, and I will succeed.**

Building Wings

"The man who has no imagination has no wings."
Muhammad Ali

When I was a child, my dad helped me build a kite that was more than six feet wide at the crossbow. It was magnificent. We bought turquoise and white material and stapled it to the frame. We made a tail from an old bedsheet. I fully expected the kite to sail to the moon, but we could barely get it off the ground. We figured out that the weight of the kite would require a monumental tail, one so long we'd never be able to launch it. But I didn't care—the making of that kite propelled the wings of my imagination nonetheless.

Today I will give my imagination a workout. Maybe I will visit a new museum, start a painting, or begin drafting a screenplay.

Glorious Miracles

"There are only two ways to live your life.
One is as though nothing is a miracle.
The other is as though everything is a miracle."

Albert Einstein

*P*ull one small flower off a bush. Look at it closely and notice the veins. Touch it gently. Smell it. Close your eyes. Try to imagine how you'd go about creating that flower. That one small flower is a miracle. So are mountains and winding rivers. When you live as if every single thing is a miracle, you live with gratitude, appreciation, and awe. It's a beautiful way to live.

Today I will marvel at every miracle I encounter.

Walking the Walk

"I love friendly deeds better than fair words."
Sir Walter Scott

air words are lovely to hear, but after a while we want action, don't we? At first we'll marvel at a good speaker and feel inspired, but if a speaker rambles on too long, we find ourselves annoyed. Not everyone can give a fair speech, but the speech is certainly easier than the hard work it takes to put our ideals into action and achieve concrete realities.

Today I resolve to do more walking than talking.

May 21

Climbing for the Truth

"In the mountains of truth, you never climb in vain. Either you already reach a higher point today, or you exercise your strength in order to be able to climb higher tomorrow."

Friedrich Nietzsche

It's true—none of our endeavors are ever really in vain. Sometimes, we gain ground. Other times, it may seem as though we are losing our footing, but these experiences make us stronger for future endeavors.

My dating experiences have been a kind of search for truth, as many endeavors in our lives are. I became a single parent in 1985, and since that time, I've dated an average of three or four men a year. Many times, the first date was also the last. (Hey, the dating game isn't so easy when you're in your 50s and 60s!) After being single for 15 years, I discovered the *zero factor*. Tony, a man I met that year, explained it to me.

"Remember high school algebra?"

I nodded just to humor him.

Tony continued, "Well, if A times B times C equals D—and if any of those first three figures is a zero—then D is going to be zero.

"If I discover someone I'm dating isn't always completely honest with me, that's a *zero factor* for me. Even if she is fabulous in all other areas—because of that zero factor—the relationship is still a zero for me."

I started making a list of characteristics that I consider to be zero factors: dishonesty, prejudice, not active enough, talks about an ex too much, boring, intellectually challenged, no sense of humor, substance abuse, no spiritual sense. Any one characteristic would be enough for me to end the relationship.

I know I have more than a few zero factors of my own to work on: gossiping, overeating, selfishness, laziness, and missing church some Sundays. These are my struggles as I inch up the mountain.

Today I will work on eliminating my zero factors. I will ride my bike at least ten miles and I will get my five servings of fruits and vegetables.

Light Up the World

"We may divide thinkers into those who think for themselves and those who think through others; the latter are the rule, the former the exception. Only the light which we have kindled in ourselves can illuminate others."

Arthur Schopenhauer

The light we have inside ourselves is our own talent, our own strength—the element that sets us apart from everyone else. We must find that element and set it afire; this is how our world lights up with energy, action, and progress. If we all depended on the lights of others, there would be no light at all.

Today I will embrace all original thoughts and ideas.

Growing Older with Grace

"When young, rejoice in the tranquility of the old."

Nagarjuna

One of my favorite things to do is organize a gathering of all my favorite elders and go out for Chinese food. I can usually come up with eight or ten oldsters and a few "youngsters" to do the driving. Most of the oldsters are in their late 70s or 80s, and a few have entered their 90s. We giggle, gab, and eat with gusto, and then we take turns reading our fortune-cookie messages. Quite honestly, I get more zest for my future from my older friends than I do from the fortune cookies.

Today I will take an older acquaintance out for coffee, and I will marvel at her wisdom and experience.

Bending Gracefully

"In flood time, you can see how some trees bend, and because they bend, even their twigs are safe, while stubborn trees are torn up, roots and all."

Sophocles

In life, we have to choose our battles—we need to be able to distinguish the significant from the trivial. That idea you threw out at last week's meeting? Maybe the idea the next person threw out was indeed stronger or timelier. Let it go, and work to incorporate your associate's idea. Next time, maybe your associate will work all the harder to incorporate yours.

Today I will be objective. If a course of action seems superior to one I had previously favored, I will go along with the new plan.

Falling Off the Bike

"You always pass failure on the way to success."
Mickey Rooney

Who among us learned to ride a bike without falling off at least once or twice? Who among us learned to parallel park without scraping the back tires on the curb? I cooked the paper bag of giblets inside the bird before I ever cooked a perfect turkey. I also tortured my folks with a thousand renditions of mindless one-finger songs before I could really play the piano. Success takes work.

Today I will not get discouraged if I find myself on the brink of failure. I will forge on.

The Meaning of Success

*"Success usually comes to those who are
too busy to be looking for it."*

Henry David Thoreau

*M*ost people who end up being successful weren't looking for success, per se. Take Bill Gates. He is now one of the most powerful people in the world. In the beginning, he was just a kid fascinated by computers. Success is fleeting; the important thing is to immerse yourself in work that you love.

Today I will focus on my work and on my passions. I will not worry about success.

Talent Show

"A genuine talent finds its way."
Johann Wolfgang von Goethe

A genuine talent cannot be stifled for long. Think of the individuals who had limited formal training but nonetheless found their niche and managed to shine: Paul Gauguin, Dorothy West, James Dean, and Mike Royko, for instance. Talent is part of an individual's very being. If we ignore or try to stifle our talent, it will keep rising up until it gets out in some form, whether we become a star in our own right or a prominent instructor for another. Why waste any time? Figure out what your talent is, then use it and enjoy it.

Today I will reflect upon my talents and abilities. If I am not making the most of them, I will find a way to do so.

May 28

Coming Attractions

"Let's tell our young people that the best books are yet to be written; the best paintings have not yet been painted; the best governments are yet to be formed; the best is yet to be done by them."

John Erskine

If a person from the 1700s could visit our world, would they not be amazed? Of course they would be. The world of the future will be just as amazing. We have to encourage our young people to dream and to work hard to make those dreams a reality.

Today I will encourage my son, daughter, niece, nephew, grandchild, or neighbor. I will make it clear that I have faith in the capabilities of their generation.

The Ride of Your Life

*"No, you never get any fun out of
the things you haven't done."*

Thomas Nash

I've had a lot of fun in my life. I've gone on a cruise, and ridden on a hot air balloon and on top of an elephant. I've enjoyed sleds, saucers, toboggans, snowmobiles, ice skates, and downhill and cross-country skis. I've in-line skated and tried out a go-kart, a surfboard, a wave runner, a water slide, and numerous amusement park rides. There's a lot I still haven't done, though. I still want to go parasailing and experience the Chunnel. Dreaming about something and actually doing it are as different as sitting on a bench watching someone else shoot down a water slide and actually doing it yourself. No comparison.

Today I will stop dreaming about parasailing and I'll make reservations to actually do it.

May 30

Be an Innovator

*"Whatever the mind of man can
conceive, it can achieve."*

W. Clement Stone

*I*nnovators the world over have proven that if
you can think it, you can do it. Think of the
inventions that we take for granted every day, from
the wheel to the lightbulb to the airplane and every
machine in between. One of my favorites is the
bicycle. I ride mine at least 10 miles a day, three
days a week. In my mind, there's no better way to
get around.

**Today if I find myself frustrated by a situation, I
will try to come up with an innovative solution.**

A Rose Is a Rose Is a Rose

"People from a planet without flowers would think we must be mad with joy the whole time to have such things about us."

Iris Murdoch

A small bouquet of wild violets picked by a five-year-old, a bride's bouquet of daisies because he gave her one daisy on their first date, a spray of mixed garden flowers decorating the dining room table because it's their 14th anniversary—flowers do make us mad with joy. Flowers can linger in our hearts long after they wilt. They are like the sweetest words, the most loving hug, the richest chocolate, and a heavenly hammock on a sweet spring day.

Today I will give flowers to someone who least expects them.

June 1

Fixing the World

*"Fill what's empty, empty what's full,
and scratch where it itches."*

Duchess of Windsor

When I was a child, I was taught to always leave a place better than it was before I got there. If I see paper on the ground at the park, I pick it up and dispose of it. If there are dishes on the coffee table at a friend's house, I pick them up and take them to the kitchen. It's just simple common courtesy. We can't expect the world to be perfect without our help.

Today I will contribute to keeping my community orderly. As I finish my grocery shopping, I will corral any carts I come across in the lot.

Wise Words

"Wisdom outweighs any wealth."

Sophocles

Wisdom is priceless. It is something that is earned over a full lifetime, and the wisdom of each individual is unique because it is achieved through a particular set of experiences and struggles. Through wisdom we earn significant riches (equanimity, respect, and the ability to reach out and help others), but riches cannot buy us wisdom.

Today I will focus on cultivating my mind. I will research a topic that has perhaps intimidated me in the past.

June 3

Shared Joy

*"Grief can take care of itself, but to get the full value
of joy you must have somebody to divide it with."*

Mark Twain

What's the first thing you do after experiencing a surprise joyful moment alone? Most of us take a picture or rush to call and describe it to a loved one. Humans are definitely social creatures; sure, experiencing a beautiful moment is a delicious treat in and of itself, but we also long to share it.

Today I will ask a friend to do something with me. Perhaps we'll go on a bike ride and marvel at all the beautiful sights.

Do It Yourself

"There are no secrets to success. It is the result of preparation, hard work, and learning from failure."

Colin Powell

Get-rich-quick schemes are enticing, but even as we listen to them there's a part of us—deep inside—that knows they can't be true, right? If it were that easy, everyone would be rich. We have learned from our own experiences and those of others that the only tried-and-true way to get ahead is to have goals and to work hard to achieve them.

Today I will reflect upon my goals and dreams for a little while, and then I will get to work.

Enthusiasm Moves Mountains

"Nothing is so contagious as enthusiasm;
it moves stones, it charms brutes.
Enthusiasm is the genius of sincerity,
and truth accomplishes no victories without it."
Edward George Bulwer-Lytton

Enthusiasm is necessary for any significant undertaking, isn't it? For everyday tasks, determination and discipline suffice, but anything out of the ordinary requires enthusiasm.

Consider D-Day for a moment. Like any great battle in history, it was, on the surface, crazy. Those soldiers were swarming onto fortified enemy territory. The only thing that propelled each soldier, one after the other, to keep landing on those beaches and to keep going after the landing was enthusiasm about the mission.

Think about any politician or anyone who runs a not-for-profit agency. They must be enthusiastic in order to get anyone to follow them, right? The politician or agency head must believe in their work; they must believe that their work is making a difference, and they must be able to spread their enthusiasm to other people. Otherwise, no one would bother.

A similar thing could be said about our own lives. Determination and discipline will get us through our daily tasks, but to accomplish our true goals and dreams—which will take planning, perseverance, and work—we must be enthused and find a way to maintain that enthusiasm.

Today I will remind myself of my goals and dreams, and I will be enthusiastic as I work toward them.

June 6

Strength of Character

*"Greatness lies not in being strong,
but in the right use of strength."*

Henry Ward Beecher

If we are merely strong, what good does it do us or anyone else? Or if we prove our strength by throwing our weight around and using it randomly, without much thought, our strength is likely overshadowed by our bad judgment. On D-Day the soldiers put on a show of great strength, but they did it only as a last resort and for an admirable cause—to defend a besieged country and a threatened world.

Today I will honor the right use of strength, and I resolve to dedicate my talents and abilities toward honorable endeavors.

Fulfillment

"That is happiness; to be dissolved into
something complete and great."

Willa Cather

Artists tend to lose themselves in their work. I've watched my oldest child paint. She squints, turns her head, and adds touches here and there. Though I've been watching her for several minutes, she is unaware of my presence. I've watched my dad at his workbench, pencil stuck over his ear. He measures, scribbles, and runs a piece of wood through the electric table saw. He is also lost in his work. The lucky ones are those whose work makes them melt into their projects so completely that the rest of the world disappears. That is happiness and fulfillment.

Today I will reflect upon whether or not I ever lose myself in my work or my hobbies. If I don't, I will embark upon a more fulfilling career or find a more suitable hobby.

June 8

We All Long for Love

*"Love and the hope of it are not things
one can learn; they are a part of life's heritage."*

Maria Montessori

*L*ove is like a sense, isn't it? It isn't something we learn about from others or at school and then long for—though of course we do learn aspects about it from others. Even the tiniest babies sense love. Sometimes newborns cry because they are hungry or wet, but often they just want to be held.

Today I will reach out to another person, whether it is my soul mate, a family member, a neighbor, or a coworker. I will comfort another and find comfort for myself as well.

Technicolor World

"It's all a matter of keeping my eyes open."
Annie Dillard

The world is an amazing place—it is just a matter of paying attention. During my outdoor water aerobics class today, I spotted a gorgeous blue heron. My eyes followed its flight until it landed on the roof behind me, and I watched as it made himself comfortable in the corner near the rainspout. I marveled at the magnificent creature and felt lucky to have had such a close-up view.

Today, I will get out there and pay attention—I don't want to miss a thing.

Sticking to it

*"Commitment is what transforms
a promise into reality."*

George Hopkins

Commitments run the gamut—from a commitment to ourselves (perhaps in the form of a New Year's resolution) to a commitment to another person (perhaps in the form of a wedding ring). Commitments can be scary, can't they? We put off making commitments because we are afraid someone might actually—gasp!—call us on them. Commitments can be hard, and they often involve sacrifice on our part. But the only way to achieve anything significant is to commit ourselves to it. If we never make any commitments, we never do anything significant; we never make any real, lasting connections. Commitments are beautiful because they are proof of a full life.

Today I will think before giving my word, but if I give it, my word will be gold.

Laugh 'Til Your Sides Ache

*"Trouble came knocking,
but hearing laughter hurried away."*
Benjamin Franklin

When in our lives have we gotten into true, regrettable trouble? More often than not, it is during unhappy times, when we do not feel hopeful. Just as the drug dealer seeks out unhappy, vulnerable people, trouble often finds those who are already feeling a little lost. If we focus on the positive and work from there, we have hope, and we smile and laugh. Positive people would often not even tend to see "trouble" as trouble; positive people would see it as a temporary problem and would quickly run it out of town.

Today I will focus on the positive, and I will have hope for my future.

June 12

Failure Is Not an Option

"Act as though it were impossible to fail."
Ralph Waldo Emerson

Have you ever been in the presence of a forceful, successful person? They appear confident and immune to failure. They keep plugging along, no matter what. If anyone around them expresses hesitation, the successful leader either does not notice or appears baffled by the hesitation. Even when such people do fail, they do not get discouraged and do not acknowledge the failure. They simply move on toward a slightly adjusted goal.

Today I will scoff at failure, and I will forge ahead.

Knowledge at Our Fingertips

"When so rich a harvest is before us, why do we not gather it? All is in our hands if we will but use it."

Elizabeth Ann Seton

The Internet immediately came to my mind when I read this quote. It amazes me every day. The possibilities are endless; it is possible to research any topic at any time. One day each week—instead of watching soap operas or another reality TV show—why don't we spend our time learning something new?

Today, I promise to move away from the TV and explore a new topic on the Internet. I feel smarter and more energized already.

Consider Your Legacy

*"Let us endeavor so to live that when we come
to die even the undertaker will be sorry."*

Mark Twain

When you think back over the history of the world, which individuals do you wish were still with us? Leaders such as Martin Luther King Jr. and Princess Diana, who gave selflessly for others; artists such as Michelangelo, Wolfgang Amadeus Mozart, Audrey Hepburn, or Jimi Hendrix? Endeavor to emulate the qualities that such individuals had. Do you want to leave your art behind? Start a new project today. Do you want to leave a legacy of goodwill and compassion? Sign up to volunteer or research ways to start a nonprofit. Live the life you so admire.

Today I resolve to embark upon a more remarkable, admirable chapter in my life.

Follow Your Heart

*"A good heart is better
than all the heads in the world."*

Edward Bulwer-Lytton

An idea that comes from our heads can lead us on a path of greed or corruption, but an idea that springs from our hearts will never do so. A "good" head can merely signify smarts and guile, but a good heart signifies altruism and sacrifice. Good heads can go awry, but a good heart never will.

Today I will heed my mind and my heart, but when they are in conflict, my heart will always win out.

June 16

Hear No Evil, See No Evil

"My life has been happy because I have had wonderful friends and plenty of interesting work to do. I seldom think about my limitations, and they never make me sad. Perhaps there is just a touch of yearning at times, but it is vague, like a breeze among flowers. The wind passes, and the flowers are content."

Helen Keller

Most of us cannot even fathom what life was like for Helen Keller. A childhood illness left her unable to see or hear, but these obstacles did not deter Keller. She went on to obtain a bachelor's degree, helped found the American Civil Liberties Union (ACLU), and was a tireless writer and lecturer. She took her life for what it was and made the most of it. This is all any of us can do, for we all have limitations and a specific set of circumstances, talents, and abilities.

Today I will make the most of my circumstances and opportunities.

Life Is a Roller Coaster

"As for the future: I'll go on believing there is one—maybe even a happy one…Whatever it may be, one thing is for sure—this adventure is not over."

Lauren Bacall

*L*ife is, most definitely, an adventure. Sometimes the adventure feels like a nightmare, sometimes like a dream come true. It's the ups and downs that make life so interesting. During the sad or trying times, we need to keep the good times in mind and have hope that all will come right again. This will give us the strength to endure and not give in. There is a rhythm to this thing called life—a sort of roller-coaster effect. And all of it taken together adds up to one grand adventure.

Today I will be ready for anything that life throws at me.

The Artist in All of Us

*"I am always doing that which I cannot do,
in order that I may learn how to do it."*

Pablo Picasso

This is the attitude to have, isn't it? Instead of doing all the things we're good at over and over (just to make us feel good about ourselves), we should keep working at the things that do not come so naturally to us. We need to challenge ourselves. Think of the feeling of accomplishment that will follow once we prove to ourselves that we actually can do the thing we thought we could not do. What are we afraid of? That others will laugh at us? Everyone who's laughing has something they're afraid to do—they just never do it.

Today I will practice the thing I think I cannot do. I will scoff at laughter (or at least laugh too) until I get it right.

Some Perspective

*"It's a recession when your neighbor
loses his job: it's a depression when you lose yours."*
Harry S. Truman

The United States hasn't had a depression since before World War II. The last depression was from May 1937 to June 1938, when the gross domestic product (GDP) declined by 18.2 percent. During our latest recession, GDP has declined by 3.4 percent. Perspective helps right now, doesn't it? Losing our heads doesn't help, though of course we must act smartly right now. We must pay our bills, and we shouldn't shop 'til we drop.

Today I will make sure all my purchases are needs, not merely wants.

June 20

The Rules of Engagement

"Don't walk in front of me, I may not follow;
don't walk behind me, I may not lead;
walk beside me, and be my friend."

Albert Camus

think every marriage ceremony should include
the above words. Neither person in a healthy
relationship should be the leader, and neither
person should be the follower—the two individuals
should be equals. They should make decisions
together, raise any children together, and socialize
together—though not all the time, of course. It is
healthy to have outlets that are all your own and
that preserve your individuality. Just make sure
you have enough in common to preserve your
bond as well.

**Today I will cherish my soul mate, and I will give
him or her the necessary space to be their own
person.**

Red Rover, Red Rover

"Youth is, after all, just a moment, but it is the moment, the spark that you always carry with you."

Raisa Gorbachev

I can still remember the jiggly feeling in my stomach as I bounced to 1,000 on my new pogo stick. I remember the first time Dad and I biked all the way to my cousin's farm—five miles! With amazing clarity, I can call to mind the act of twisting the nut on my clamp-on roller skates with my big metal skate key. And I remember how my feet tickled in those skates when I whizzed over the cracks in the sidewalk. I sometimes have trouble remembering what I did yesterday, but I remember my youth with indelible detail.

Today I will do something from my childhood. I'll jump in the waves of the Gulf, play jacks, or toss a water balloon at a friend.

The Joy of a Good Laugh

"The most wasted of all days is one without laughter."

e. e. cummings

Why are we here? Generations of people have asked that question, and we all come to our own conclusions. I think the most obvious reason is to live and just enjoy the adventure. Why not take a moment each day to just smile, laugh, and relish life? It is a beautiful thing.

I know I will have an opportunity to laugh today, and I will take it.

Beautiful Treasures

"A thing of beauty is a joy forever."
John Keats

*D*o you possess something that you hold on to simply because you treasure its beauty? I do. My grandmother died when my mother was just 11, so I never knew my grandmother. I do, however, know that she was a brilliant woman—a college math and physics professor. Her hobby was wood burning, and I have the wooden jewelry box on which she burned delicate flowers, winding leaves, and an intricate butterfly. That jewelry box is one of my most treasured possessions. The fact that my grandmother made it with her own two hands makes it positively exquisite.

I will take special notice of each beautiful thing that I come across today.

June 24

What Lies Within

*"What lies behind us and what lies before us
are small matters compared to what lies within us."*

Ralph Waldo Emerson

Most creatures just go about their days addressing their immediate needs, but humans are different. We take in and process our surroundings, and we have magnificent imaginations that allow us to come up with creative solutions to any problems we come across. The nitty-gritty that lies deep within our souls gives us our unique essence. What lies within us is all the strength, compassion, forgiveness, loyalty, talent, humor, and passion we need. It's all there, inside us, waiting to be ignited. Start your engines!

Today I will take stock of my personal strengths, and I will put them to use.

Learning from Each Other

"It is through generating stories of our own crisis and hope and telling them to one another that we light the path."

Rosemary Radford Reuther

Telling our own stories is cathartic, but it also helps others. Sometimes the only way we can make it through the most difficult circumstances is by looking to the examples of others and gaining strength and courage from them. We must share and help each other, for most everyone will need to gain strength from others at some point in their lives.

Today I will listen to others' stories, and I will offer insight into my own struggles when appropriate.

June 26

Gentle Strength

*"Nothing is so strong as gentleness,
nothing so gentle as real strength."*

Francis de Sales

When we are angered and tempted to use our inherent strength, it takes even more strength to resist that impulse, doesn't it? It takes more strength to be gentle and clear-minded in such circumstances. When we remain in control, our strength speaks volumes. Think of a parent who is angered over a child's behavior. A parent completely losing it is not handling the situation constructively. If the parent remains in control and manages to be both firm and gentle, however, the parent is setting a magnificent example.

Today I will remain in control, even if I feel provoked. I will be both strong and gentle.

Talking Too Much

"Blessed is the man who, having nothing to say, abstains from giving wordy evidence of the fact."
George Eliot

Isn't silence refreshing sometimes? Many of us modern humans seem to need constant stimulation. Do you ever find yourself trying to listen to the news and catch up on your e-mails at the same time? One of the tasks is sure to suffer. Many of us feel a constant need to be busy, but it is in the silent moments that we have time to really process all that has happened to us during a given day.

Today I will speak only when I have something useful to say. I will not talk just to fill the silence.

Fear Be Gone

*"Only when we are no longer afraid
do we begin to live."*

Dorothy Thompson

I live along the west coast of Florida, and swimming in the Gulf is one of my favorite activities. A fear of sharks kept me from the water until I learned that from 1995 to 2005, there were (on average) only six fatal shark attacks worldwide each year. So now I focus on my love of swimming, and I forget about the sharks. It's all mind over matter, and I don't want to let fear keep me from getting out there and enjoying my life.

Today I will not be afraid.

The Artist's World

*"I cannot help it that my paintings do not sell.
The time will come when people will see
that they are worth more than the price of the paint."*

Vincent van Gogh

Having faith in yourself is imperative. Have you written a book, but you're having a devil of a time selling it? Send it to another publisher, even if you've already sent it to three dozen. Have you created a sculpture or piece of jewelry, but you can't find anyone to buy or market it? Keep creating, and keep marketing your pieces yourself. Have faith in your work. Even if it doesn't sell in your lifetime, who cares? At least you will have lived a happy, fulfilling life. Some of the world's most gifted artists never sold a piece of work in their lifetimes. Art lives in its own sphere, forever.

**Today I will keep creating and doing what I love.
I will not get discouraged.**

June 30

"He is rich who is content with the least;
for contentment is the wealth of nature."

Socrates

Why do people travel great distances to see beautiful natural vistas for themselves? I think it is the calming effect the sights have on us. We feel serene, awed, and content. Nature is content, isn't it? A regal redwood isn't trying to be a dashing rose—the redwood just stands tall, content to be a redwood. Ah, if we could only be content to be exactly what we are. For what we are deep inside is just as beautiful, if not more so, because of what we are capable of doing with it through our minds. Many of us are awed by those stories about the young man who starts in the company mailroom and ends up as the CEO by the time he's 40. But who's to say the man who will make history is any happier than the stock clerk, the dishwasher, or the janitor? Maybe the stock clerk has a beautiful family, tons of friends, and is a dozen times happier than the CEO who is no longer thrilled by his mansion or his Mercedes.

Today I will be happy just being me.

Beauty All Around Us

"A rock pile ceases to be a rock pile
the moment a single man contemplates it,
bearing within him the image of a cathedral."

Antoine de Saint-Exupéry

There's an old story about a traveler who comes across three bricklayers. The traveler asks the first man, "What are you doing?" The bricklayer shrugs and says dryly, "I'm earning my wage." The traveler asks the second bricklayer, "What are you doing, sir?" That man shrugs, "Me? I'm building a wall." Then the traveler asks the last bricklayer what he's doing. The man turns around, flashes a huge smile, and says, "Sir, I am building a marvelous cathedral." Life is a matter of perspective.

Today I will find the beauty in everyday things.

Laughing Yourself Well

"Optimism supplies the basic energy of civilization. Optimism doesn't wait on facts. It deals with prospects. Pessimism is a waste of time."

Norman Cousins

*N*orman Cousins, who edited *Saturday Review* for more than 30 years, was a great fan of laughter. After he was diagnosed with a life-threatening form of arthritis, he checked himself out of the hospital and into a hotel. He hired a nurse to take a sample of his blood, and then he laughed. He laughed every day over and over while watching funny films and listening to funny albums. He wanted only funny people in his room. He and his nurse conducted an experiment and discovered that after five minutes of genuine belly laughter, his immune system cells increased in number and activity by 50 percent. Cousins turned pessimism into gold-plated optimism. He lived and laughed for 26 more years.

Today I will laugh at my aches and pains, and I will begin to banish any pessimism from my being.

Pull Me Up

*"There are two ways of exerting one's strength:
One is pushing down; the other is pulling up."*

Booker T. Washington

If we are strong, we have a responsibility to use that gift to lift those around us rather than pushing them further down to make us feel better about ourselves. Besides, when anyone succeeds, it usually lifts everyone around them a little bit too.

Today I will make an effort to help those who have less than I do.

July 4

The Fruits of Dreams

"Throw your dreams into space like a kite,
and you do not know what it will bring back—
a new life, a new friend, a new love, a new country."

Anaïs Nin

The best part of life is that we don't have to have the same life day after day, month after month, year after year. If we are determined enough, we can change and improve our lives at any time. Follow your dreams, and beautiful things will come your way if you take the time to notice them. What is your dream? Will it involve travel, new friends, or a new love? Only time will tell.

Today I will make progress on a dream, and I will embrace all the fruits of it.

One Small Step

"We must be the change we wish to see in the world."
Mohandas Gandhi

Sometimes the problems of the world seem daunting, but we must remember that change starts with us. We will not begin to notice positive changes until we change our own attitude and ourselves. We all become saddened and depressed at times, but despair is not constructive. What about the world is most depressing to you? That people are homeless? Volunteer at a shelter or donate to one. Make the small changes that are within your reach, and you will begin to notice positive changes in the world.

Today I will take stock of my specific community, and I will find a way to contribute to making it better.

July 6

Embrace Today

"While one person hesitates because he feels inferior, another person is busy making mistakes and becoming superior."

Henry C. Link

Self-esteem is something built over time by many different experiences. If we are lovingly cared for as a baby and given encouragement as a child, we are more likely to value ourselves. Healthy people do not feel inferior to others—they are just aware that all people have different talents and interests. Some people are gifted artists, some have a flair for numbers, some are brilliant scientists, and some are compassionate caregivers. We should never let an inferiority complex hold us back. What are we afraid of? That we might make a mistake? Go for it. We all make mistakes—smart, healthy people learn from them and move on instead of wallowing in self-pity.

Today is a new day, and I embrace it with love in my heart. I forgive myself for my past mistakes, and I begin my future with my self-esteem intact.

Sparks of Beauty

"A morning-glory at my window satisfies me more than the metaphysics of books."

Walt Whitman

Even when we are down, a spark of beauty has the power to astonish us and startle us right out of our funk. We just have to pay attention.

Today I will pay attention. I will not let one spark of beauty pass me by.

July 8

Time Spent with Friends

"Stay is a charming word in a friend's vocabulary."
Louisa May Alcott

The first clue someone loves us is if he or she seems to want us around, right? Spending time together brings comfort to both parties—it is nice to be comforted, of course, but it is also nice to be needed. When we realize a friend needs us, it is a beautiful feeling.

Today I will invite a friend over for coffee or tea. When she goes to gather her things, I will ask her to please stay for a second cup.

Detours Can Be Delightful

*"A good traveler has no fixed plans,
and is not intent on arriving."*

Lao Tzu

*T*he travelers on this road of life must have a rough plan, but we all know what happens to the best-laid plans. We must enjoy the little thrills we encounter along the way, and we need to be open to detours on a moment's notice. Sometimes the best experiences occur along those detours, don't they?

Today I will embrace each detour and all its possibilities.

July 10

Move On

*"A wise man will make haste to forgive,
because he knows the true value of time, and will
not suffer it to pass away in unnecessary pain."*

Samuel Johnson

Forgiveness is hard, but delaying it only prolongs the painful moments. Always be understanding and ready to forgive, for each of us has needed forgiveness in the past and will need it again in the future. Make peace, and move on to the next chapter of your life.

Today I will be ready to promptly forgive.

Stretchy, Stretchy, Ahhhhhhh

"I base my fashion taste on what doesn't itch."

Gilda Radner

*L*ife's too short to be uncomfortable. I have a few rules of my own: no choking necklines, no high heels, no pantyhose, no belts, nothing that pulls, feels tight, or forces me to hold in my stomach. Also, no brand advertisements; goofy sayings; or flower, butterfly, or birdhouse pictures that make me look ancient. I dress for comfort, pure and simple.

Today I will dress for comfort, and I will carry myself proudly. A smile and really good posture are the best fashion accessories.

July 12

Anger Danger

*"Speak when you are angry
and you will make the best speech
you will ever regret."*

Ambrose Bierce

I used to think the person who walked away from a good argument was a fool, but I now know the person who walks away is very wise. When you feel the blood rushing to your face, think very carefully—the words that come to your mouth may be life-altering. Do you really want to blurt out what you are thinking at that very moment? Aren't your thoughts more akin to those of a possessed person? We remember things that hurt us to the core for a lifetime. Do you really want to rattle off a slew of hurtful words at this person? Do you really want to hear every thought anyone has ever had about you? Keep your mouth closed, and walk away. You can always have a discussion later, when you are back to your true, more generous self.

If I feel angry today, I will take deep breaths—and through my *nose*. I will not open the volcano that is my mouth.

Find Your Why

*"He who has a why to live for can
bear almost any how."*

Friedrich Nietzsche

Life is hard, isn't it? Even if our basic needs are met, there are other circumstances that make our lives difficult. Perhaps we hate our jobs, so we feel all our time is spent doing tedious or pointless things. Or perhaps we live stressfully from paycheck to paycheck. But isn't there some bright spot in your life that makes it all worth it? Maybe you're lucky enough to be a talented artist, and you love your work. Or maybe you would do absolutely anything in the world for your loved ones. The trick is to find your why and keep it in sight.

Today I will ponder my why. If it is a dream I haven't attained, I will work tirelessly toward it.

July 14

Practice Makes Perfect

*"It's a funny thing,
the more I practice the luckier I get."*

Arnold Palmer

Some people don't believe in luck, and it seems that Arnold Palmer is one of these people. He knows how hard he has worked, and he credits this with his success. Luck may be the reason behind some things (winning the lottery, for instance), but those glories pale in comparison to what hard work and practice can bring us.

Today I will work hard, and I will improve.

What We Don't Know

"All truth passes through three stages.
First, it is ridiculed. Second, it is violently opposed.
Third, it is accepted as being self-evident."

Arthur Schopenhauer

We can be cynical at times. We live in such a modern age, and we have all kinds of information at our fingertips; sometimes we forget that there's actually a lot we *don't* know. Are there planets that are capable of sustaining life? Who knows, maybe future generations will *live* on other planets. We need to be open to new ideas and new ways of thinking.

Today I will do some research before I make up my mind about an issue.

July 16

How to Get Stuff

*"The indispensable first step to getting the things
you want out of life is this: Decide what you want."*

Ben Stein

Many of us run around in circles all day, and
then complain that we never have time to
address *our* needs or *our* wants. What is it you
want or need? More time with your kids or time to
take classes to pursue a dream? Do you desire more
time for travel, or to work out, or to get a massage
or other treat? Figure out what you want, and come
up with a plan to work toward it. Discuss your
dream with others—you may be pleasantly surprised
at who's willing to pitch in to help you achieve it.

**Today I will get up early and complete my workout
for the day. This will give me more relaxing time
with loved ones tonight.**

All Used Up

"I want to be all used up when I die."

George Bernard Shaw

Are we too careful? Do we save too much money? Squirrel away too many nuts for the winter? Do we put things off until "later"? If we really want to be all used up when we die, we need to take chances and have more adventures. We need to start doing the things we plan to do "someday."

Today I am going to ponder my dreams and start working toward one.

The Power of You

*"Trust yourself. You know more
than you think you do."*

Benjamin Spock

How is it that a mother can look at her
child and know if he or she is really sick?
How is it that a person can sense when a loved
one is happy, sad, or angry without a word being
spoken? Instinct—the power we all have within
ourselves. Trust yourself. You know what to do.

Today I will heed my instincts.

Pleasing All the People

"I don't know the key to success,
but the key to failure is trying to please everybody."
Bill Cosby

We all have different opinions and ideas, and that is what keeps the world so interesting. Trying to be a people-pleaser is a no-win situation. First of all, in doing so, we find ourselves rolled so thin it becomes difficult to hold ourselves together. Also, if it becomes clear to others that we are only aiming to please, people lose respect for us because there is nothing definitive about us that sets us apart from everyone else. We need to get used to the fact that sometimes, other people are not going to be happy with us. We must do what we think is right and not worry so much about what others think.

Today if I displease someone, I will stop and consider what occurred. If I feel certain I did nothing wrong, I will simply let it go.

July 20

Sticking to It

*"Strength does not come from winning.
Your struggles develop your strengths.
When you go through hardships and decide
not to surrender, that is strength."*

Arnold Schwarzenegger

Think back over the times when you have really noticed your own strength. It wasn't from winning, was it? Oftentimes we win because our opponent is simply not very good. The times we witness our own strength is when we are pushed very hard. When I first became a single parent, things were very difficult. When I realized I could actually handle it, though, it was a gratifying feeling. I felt like I could conquer the world if I had to.

Today I will not quit, no matter what. I know I can succeed.

Professor Experience

"Trust one who has gone through it."

Virgil

If you're about to embark upon significant work on your house, whom do you call for advice? A friend or neighbor who has had similar work done recently, right? It should be the same way with any project or problem we face. If we are sick or grieving, wouldn't it help to go to a friend or family member who has gone through something similar in the past? We don't have to confront every problem alone. It is not weak to seek out help and advice—it is wise. Besides, when we reach out to others, we strengthen our bonds with them. Perhaps they will come to us for advice in the future.

If I am daunted by any task or problem today, I will rack my brain to try to think of someone who could help or offer advice.

Clearing the Mind

"Rest is not idleness, and to lie sometimes on the grass under trees on a summer's day, listening to the murmur of the water, or watching the clouds float across the sky, is by no means a waste of time."

Sir John Lubbock

A beautiful summer's day is the perfect time to just be outside and enjoy it—just look around you and smile. Do not make a mental note of your grocery list; do not think about your personal problems or work problems. Just take it all in. We all need times like these to clear our heads and remember why it's all worth it.

I will carve out some time in this gorgeous summer day to simply sit and enjoy all the beauty around me.

The Blessing of One True Friend

"If you have one true friend,
you have more than your share."

Thomas Fuller

*D*o you have one true friend? A person you just know you can count on no matter what? Someone you know would be there for you at your darkest hour or during a time of desperate need? Acquaintances come and go, but the spark and dedication of a true friend is a treasure.

Today I will call my true friend and thank her for all she adds to my life.

Thrill of Discovery

"The real voyage of discovery consists not in seeking new landscapes but in having new eyes."

Marcel Proust

Preconceived notions are dangerous, aren't they? When we have them, we miss a lot. Take your ride to work, for example. Do you look around on your way, or are you just focused on your destination? Do you have the mind-set of "Oh, I see this every day—it's nothing special"? Take time to look around you with the eyes of a newcomer. You will be amazed at the beauty you've overlooked all along.

As I go about my day, I will try to have the mind-set of the first person ever to walk along these paths.

Hear, See, Do

*"I hear and I forget.
I see and I understand. I do and I remember."*

Confucius

*M*any years ago, a friend told me how much she enjoyed painting ceramics. It didn't sound that interesting to me, so I *forgot* about it completely. Years later I wandered into a ceramics place with another friend, and we saw dinner plates made out of greenware. Now I began to *understand* how I could have fun painting ceramics. A few years later, I finally decided to give it a try. Now—dozens of plates later—I've become passionate about painting them. I am thankful for this new hobby that brings me joy, invigorates my mind, and strengthens my creativity.

Today I will pursue an activity that I've only heard about before.

July 26

Little Things, Big Results

"The smallest fact is a window through which the infinite may be seen."

Aldous Huxley

*H*ave you ever noticed how pondering one thing leads to pondering numerous others? Take the time to really examine a beautiful flower, and your mind will come up with one question after another. What components came together to create this beautiful plant? Why does it look the way it does? It is amazing. Small things enlarge and excite our world.

Today I will notice and marvel at the tiniest facts.

The Ultimate Test

"The true measure of a man is how he treats someone who can do him absolutely no good."

Samuel Johnson

*N*etworking is big these days. Business professionals get together at seven-too-early-o'clock in the morning to strut their stuff. They pass out dozens of business cards and relate how *their* business can help *your* business. But the real test of what we're worth is how we treat the janitor, the cashier at the grocery store, the little children on our block, or the old couple down the street. Are we simply after our own interests, or are our lives more meaningful?

Today I will treat all I encounter with respect.

July 28

Friendship Sparklers

"At times, our own light goes out and is rekindled by a spark from another person."

Albert Schweitzer

Once my children were grown, I decided I didn't like cooking anymore. I worked out a nice arrangement with my friend Jack, who lives just 57 steps from my condo. He agreed to cook once or twice a week if I cooked once or twice a week; the other days we would fend for ourselves, eat leftovers together, or go out to eat. Then I met Surinder, a delightful woman who teaches cooking classes in her home. The classes were magical, and the food was so delicious, it rekindled my interest in following recipes and making my own magic in the kitchen. Surinder was the spark I needed to try new flavors, tastes, and textures. Life is delicious once again.

Today I will allow someone to be a spark for me, or I will endeavor to be a spark for another.

All the Big and Little Ways

*"There is no point at which you can say,
'Well, I'm successful now. I might as well take a nap.'"*

Carrie Fisher

No matter how successful we are, there's always more to be done, isn't there? Even if our career has been a success and we are nearing retirement, we still want to be of use. We all take vacations or days off, but those days usually just recharge us; soon we are looking for meaningful work again. Everyone wants to be of use, whether it's an older person who may not be able to get around much anymore but has plenty of wisdom and life experience or a child who is ready for only the smallest tasks. We all see work to be done and long for that feeling of accomplishment.

Today I will attend to the needs around me, and I will savor the feeling of accomplishment my work brings.

A Beautiful Life

"Beauty is but a flower, which wrinkles will devour."
Thomas Nash

I was recently standing in line at the grocery checkout, feeling glum about my crow's-feet, gray hair, and my gone-with-the-wind figure, which had gone from Scarlett to Mammy in the space of a decade. I picked up a magazine with alluring headlines: "Get Gorgeous!" "Look 10 lbs Thinner!" "Fabulous at 50!"

I opened the magazine and flipped through the pages: "Amazing diet turns ugly fat into harmless water and flows it right out of your system. Works so fast, you shrink down your waistline as much as a full size smaller in just 24 hours." *Hmm, no diet pills, no strenuous exercises—I've been dreaming of this for years.*

"Grow fresher, younger-looking skin while you sleep. New wrinkle-removing formula instantly takes 10 to 15 years off your face." *What if I used it twice? Why, I'd be 29 again—no more laugh lines, crow's-feet, or furrowed forehead.*

And then, the dream of mothers everywhere: "Stretch marks disappear instantly." *Could I really wear a bikini?*

I read on, daydreaming of the new me. *Would my friends be so jealous they'd never take me bowling again?*

I put the magazine back on the rack. It's really just silliness, isn't it? Spending all this time and money on our looks when we could be focusing on what really matters—creating a life by spending time with loved ones and exploring this world of ours. Obviously we all want to look nice and be as healthy as possible, but beyond that, it's pure silliness and at times borderline narcissism. Have you ever noticed truly beautiful older people? They are beautiful because of their shining eyes and ready smile—their love of life, not because they have nipped and tucked to the point where they look like caricatures of their 20-something selves.

Today I will make myself presentable (okay, I might even spend the extra 15 minutes to look really nice), and I will get out there and live my life.

July 31

Spend Your Time Wisely

"Time is the coin of your life. It is the only coin you have, and only you can determine how it will be spent. Be careful lest you let other people spend it for you."

Carl Sandburg

Your boss, your kids, your spouse, your mother, your friends, the neighbors, the PTA, your kids' teachers—they all want a chunk of your time. Being busy is good; it keeps us social and connected. Just make sure things are in balance. There are times when we agree to do something simply because a loved one asks—everything is give and take. Just be sure you're also getting to do the things *you* want to do instead of always feeling pressured to attend to everyone else's needs.

Today I will think carefully before agreeing to an activity—I will not always just say, "Sure," and then be frantic about getting everything done.

Glorious Possibilities

"The moment when first you wake up in the morning is the most wonderful of the 24 hours. No matter how weary or dreary you may feel, you possess the certainty that... absolutely anything may happen. And the fact that it practically always doesn't, matters not one jot. The possibility is always there."

Monica Baldwin

Today is a new day—it's a powerful statement, isn't it? It is simple, yet powerful and full of hope. Each new day is a do-over—a chance to do things differently. Yesterday, I may have eaten poorly, sat around instead of exercising, and been grumpy. Today can be the exact opposite.

Today is full of hope, and I will make the most of it.

August 2

Lighting Each Other's Way

*"We cannot hold a torch to light another's
path without brightening our own."*

Ben Sweetland

Sometimes we spend so much time and effort
helping other people that we worry we
are nearly ignoring our own needs. Certainly this
can become a problem, but in general, we need
not spend too much time worrying about this. In
helping others, we often find that we ourselves have
learned something or benefited as well. Perhaps we
go out of our way to help a friend, and the time
spent figuring out a problem draws us closer to
that friend. Perhaps that friend then introduces
us to a new acquaintance who ends up helping us
with a perplexing problem in the future. We can
feel secure that any chance taken to help another is
never time spent in vain.

**Today if I am able to be of service to another, I will
not hesitate to help.**

226

Now and Ever After

"The average man, who does not know what to do with his life, wants another one which will last forever."

Anatole France

Many of us live our days in fear and hesitation. We talk ourselves out of taking chances because we are afraid of all the things that *might* happen. But we are also afraid of death and what may come after, so we want our lives to last forever, even though we spend our lives not doing very much. It is a vicious circle. Jump out of it! Go after your dreams. Maybe things won't turn out quite like you hope, but you will have lived a full life, and you will have no regrets. Let's say my dream is to start a restaurant. If I love it and nurture it—if I treat it as my baby—I will likely be successful. Maybe it won't be the absolute best restaurant in town, but the people in the immediate neighborhood will love it and support it, and I will be living my dream. And if it fails, I will just pick up the pieces and move on to the next adventure.

Today I will figure out what to do with my life, and I will work toward my dreams.

The Big Goof

*"Make the mistakes of yesterday
your lessons for today."*

Theodore Roosevelt

I was recently on my way to an event at a large
retirement facility. I was to be the keynote
speaker, and I was going over everything in my
mind as I drove to the event. I had remembered
everything: my suitcase full of props, books to sell,
a tablecloth for the book table, price signs, dollar
bills for making change, flyers, business cards, and a
bottle of water. The one thing I forgot: *my speech.*

Granted, I don't use notes much, but they help keep
me on track. I refer to my notes for detailed facts,
and they pull me back to the core if I find myself
telling yet another story. For the first time in
20-plus years of giving speeches, I'd forgotten
to put my notes in my prop suitcase with my
collection of rubber chickens.

It was too late to turn back. I knew my talk was
divided into three parts, and each part had five
sections. So as I drove the car, trying to keep from
hyperventilating, I asked my sister to take notes as
I related all I could remember.

And yes, with only one-fiftieth of my notes in front of me, I delivered the speech just fine. But I also was reminded of a good lesson that day—don't fly by the seat of your pants. Take the time to make lists, and pack carefully. Even though I don't really need my security blanket that much, it's nice to have it there just in case I have a senior moment someday.

If I make a mistake today, I will figure out a lesson to learn from it.

Dare to Be Childlike

"Only the most mature of us are able to be childlike."
Madeleine L'Engle

Children see everything with new, unbiased eyes. The world is magical to them. Children are not self-conscious, and because of this, they are quite free. They do and say what is on their minds, with little thought of what others think. Once we gain wisdom through experience, we become like little children again in that respect—suddenly we are confident and free to follow our dreams, with little thought of practicality or worry about what others might think. We can engage in fancy, and feel confident that it is not silliness—it is an integral part of a full life. Instead of analyzing everything and letting inconsequential matters get us down, we can make a point to just appreciate and enjoy life.

I vow to take at least a moment out of this day to look at the world through childlike eyes.

The Measure of Life

*"Not everything that can be counted counts,
and not everything that counts can be counted."*

Albert Einstein

If we tried to count all the inconsequential things we came across each day, it would drive us batty. The number of cracks on the sidewalk; the number of stoplights we pass on our way to work; the number of beige cars we encounter—these are all countable things, but it is not worth our time to count them. There are other things, on the other hand, that really do matter, but it is impossible to count or measure them: a hug from a loved one; a child's smile; a heart-to-heart with an aging parent. Our minds cannot measure these things, but our hearts surely keep stock of them.

Today I will savor each unmeasurable joyous experience.

August 7

What Would You Do in This Case?

"Advice is seldom welcome, and those who want it the most always like it the least."

Earl of Chesterfield

Most of us want to do things our own way. We make our own mistakes, and we learn from them—this is what makes each life different. It is important to learn from the experiences of others, though, because this is what creates progress. It would be silly for all of us to keep repeating the same mistakes over and over again. Each generation builds upon the experiences and wisdom of the generations that came before.

Today I will be open to advice. I do not have to heed it, but I will listen.

Natural Talent

*"The job of an educator is to teach students
to see the vitality in themselves."*

Joseph Campbell

If a student learns everything about the universe but nothing about their own talents, what use would it be? If they don't get the connection that they can actually *apply* all that they learn, all the years of education will just add up to wasted (though intriguing) time.

Today I will be useful and productive.

How to Manage Life

"Both optimists and pessimists contribute to our society. The optimist invents the airplane and the pessimist the parachute."

Gladys Bronwyn Stern

This world needs the daring people and the careful people—the person who invented the bicycle, and the person who invented helmets, the person who invented the car, and the person who invented seatbelts. With both of them around, the world is kept in perfect balance.

Today I will endeavor to be both daring and smart.

The Badge of Courage

*"I gain strength, courage, and confidence
by every experience in which I must
stop and look fear in the face."*

Eleanor Roosevelt

When we are faced with difficult circumstances, our instinct is often to try to avoid them. Why use the energy to deal with them if you can just avoid them, right? Often, though, the circumstances keep coming back at you in different forms until you deal with them head-on. And difficult circumstances are often the ones that form our character and shape our lives. When we face them with courage and conquer them, we only grow stronger. Avoidance stunts our growth, and we grow weaker.

Today I will not cower from anything that comes my way. I will stand tall, and I will grow stronger.

August 11

Giving Wings to Wishes

"Don't make a wish—make a life."

Sonya Friedman

It's important to have wishes and dreams, but sitting around wishing and dreaming does not accomplish much. We have to give our wishes and dreams wings. We need to go to school, then to meetings, social events, and trips. We have to mix with people who have similar wishes and dreams and learn how much hard work goes into making those dreams and wishes come true.

Today I will make progress toward a wish.

Turn the Corner

"It is good to embrace a hope."

Ovid

*H*ope is what keeps us going when things are at their darkest. Hope can get us through all the hardships of life—stress, disease, disaster, a tumbling economy, and war. How do we find hope when all seems dark? We think over past experiences. Anything can happen, right? Haven't we all had times in our past when everything seemed dark, but then something wonderful happened? We know there's every possibility that that can happen again. We never know what wonderful thing awaits us if we can just turn this next corner.

Today I will keep my hopes up, no matter what.

Kindness Matters

"Kind words can be short and easy to speak, but their echoes are truly endless."

Mother Teresa

Compliments make you feel good, and giving them feels just as good as receiving them. For example, if you compliment someone's cooking, seeing their pleased reaction leaves you with a good feeling. Compliments are contagious; after someone receives a compliment, he or she feels good and is more likely to compliment someone else. And the more you compliment others, the more you begin to notice things that are worthy of compliments. Before you know it, you are in the habit of focusing on the good and the beautiful.

Today I will take every opportunity to say a kind word.

Life by Example

*"Example is not the main thing in
influencing others. It is the only thing."*

Albert Schweitzer

have always admired my dad's example. He
is now in his 90s, but his life has been one
consistent example. If he sees a scrap of paper on
the sidewalk, he picks it up and tosses it in a trash
can. In the summer, he'll bend down to pull a stray
weed from a sidewalk crack. If he sees a project
that needs doing, he's the first to volunteer. If
someone's in trouble, he's the first to stop and help.
Such a true, gentle, consistent demeanor is the best
example.

**Today I will think before I act, making sure my
example matches my ideals.**

The Economics of Trust

"If a man empties his purse into his head no one can take it away from him. An investment in knowledge always pays the best interest."

Benjamin Franklin

Money is important, but knowledge always takes us further. We need money to live, but knowledge enriches our lives. We can have all the money in the world, but if we don't know anything, what good will the money do us? Maybe we can have the most fabulous car, or the nicest house, or the most beautiful clothes, but life is empty with no interesting goals or exhilarating conversation.

Today I will make an investment in knowledge. I will sign up for a class; read an informative newspaper, magazine, or book; research a subject on the Internet; or watch a documentary.

Let's Start Now

"How wonderful it is that nobody need wait a single moment before starting to improve the world."

Anne Frank

*L*ook at the world around you—what needs to be done? Are there people in your community whose basic needs are not being met? Volunteer at a soup kitchen or donate money or goods to a shelter. Is your neighborhood park or community center looking a little worse for wear? Research ways to help. Perhaps you can set up a cleanup day on which volunteers can sign up to pick up trash, clean, or paint. We are all responsible for the condition of our neighborhoods.

Today I will do something to contribute to the upkeep of my community.

Confidently Speaking

*"I've played golf all my life so I've had lots of practice.
But so have all the other pros. The difference between
good golfers and great golfers is confidence. You've
got to believe in yourself if you're going to win."*

Lee Trevino

*N*erves get us nowhere. We have to prepare and
then believe in our capabilities and ourselves.
If we have prepared properly, why should we be
nervous? We are ready. If we let nerves take over
instead of confidence, we are giving our competitors
an advantage. So just step out there with a smile.
You're prepared, and you can do it.

**Today I will pull my shoulders back and set out
into the world with confidence.**

Stargazing

"Too low they build who build beneath the stars."
Edward Young

Why not shoot for the highest? What is your dream? Start toward it today. Have you always wanted to be a great actor? Start taking acting lessons and going out for auditions. You may or may not ever make it to Broadway, but at least you'll be living your dream.

Today I will take steps toward fulfilling my dream. Even if they're baby steps, I will be that much closer to achieving my goals.

Friendship

*"Wishing to be friends is quick work,
but friendship is a slow ripening fruit."*

Aristotle

We can't hurry anything in this life; everything really does come to fruition on its own schedule. Have you ever tried to make something happen, only to have each attempt foiled? We do have to exert some effort, but then we just have to let go and let nature take its course. For instance, if we try too hard at any relationship, we do not come off as we truly are. Think about your nearest and dearest friends; you didn't specifically choose any of them, did you? Most of us are thrown together because of circumstances, and it takes time to get to know someone—to know what they're made of, how they think, and what they like. It takes time, but a true friendship is well worth it.

Today I will take my best friend out for lunch and get to know her even better.

To Give Is to Receive

"You can get everything in life you want if you will just help enough other people get what they want."

Zig Ziglar

*I*n her book *No Greater Love,* Mother Teresa relates a story about a wealthy woman who asked how she could share in Mother Teresa's work. As the two women talked, Mother Teresa complimented the woman on her beautiful sari. The woman confessed that she sometimes spent as much as 800 rupees on one sari. Mother Teresa mentioned that her own simple sari cost only 8 rupees. She suggested that the next time the woman bought a sari, she could spend only 500 rupees and use 300 rupees to buy saris for the poor. Mother Teresa wrote, "The good woman now wears 100-rupee saris and says this has changed her life, assuring me that she has received more than what she has given."

Today I will go through my closet and find one item to donate to charity. Someone out there likely needs it more than I do.

Nobody's Perfect

"When you are offended at any man's fault,
turn to yourself and study your own failings.
Then you will forget your anger."

Epictetus

*I*t's easy to get exasperated with others, isn't it?
Most of us live in relatively close quarters, and
thus there are a lot of opportunities to let our
own needs get in the way of common courtesy and
understanding. In addition, many news sources
focus on stories about people who messed up, and
we all take turns discussing the stories and offering
our opinions. None of us are perfect, and neither is
the world. Why, then, do we make such a big deal
out of problems and disagreements? They are part
of the natural order of things. No one else is asking
for our approval, and we do not have to give it.
But being part of a community does involve having
patience when mistakes occur, whether they are our
own or someone else's.

**If I find myself annoyed with someone else today,
I will remind myself of my own imperfections and I
will be patient.**

Give It Your All

"Just do what you do best."

Red Auerbach

This is good advice. Many of us are lucky to have a lot of choices, but this makes the choosing difficult. If you do what you do best—and what you love—it is easy to be happy. If we are using our natural talents, we feel as though we are doing what we were meant to be doing.

Today I will make use of my natural talents.

Infinity and Beyond

*"If you wish to advance into the infinite,
explore the finite in all directions."*
Johann Wolfgang von Goethe

*M*any aspects of our world are a mystery to us, and sometimes it can feel overwhelming. There will always be things out of our reach, but what we can do is explore anything and everything within our reach. As we do that, more and more becomes clear, and we find more and more happiness and satisfaction.

Today I will make plans to visit a museum or an area I've never been to before.

Creative Thinking

*"The secret of success is to know
something nobody else knows."*

Aristotle Onassis

The secret of success is to figure out
something truly special and make use of it.
This takes a lot of work, study, and determination.
We ponder things every day, though; did you
ever think that maybe you just haven't looked at
something in a practical way? Think of your day-to-
day life; what is something you dread doing? Can
you think of a way to make it easier, or think of a
different way of doing it that might make it more
fun? Maybe you have come up with a system of
organizing your tax materials that you think is top-
notch. Try to market it. Be a problem-solver.

**Today I will ponder my life, and I will try to come
up with an innovative solution to a perplexing
problem.**

August 25

Blessed Screwups

"A mistake is simply another way of doing things."
Katharine Graham

When we are young, we are often admonished for our mistakes. We begin to try to avoid mistakes at all costs. But this is impossible, isn't it? Everyone makes mistakes, and for the most part, they are simply learning experiences. Mistakes can even be fun—like when you get lost and you have to ask for directions. I've met wonderful, helpful, friendly people that way. I've made huge mistakes with my cooking. Mistakes make us stretch our minds, looking for fixes, and sometimes we create a masterpiece.

If I make a mistake today, I will not get discouraged. I will keep at it until I get it right.

Choosing Your Path

"Destiny is not a matter of chance, it is a matter of choice; it is not a thing to be waited for, it is a thing to be achieved."

William Jennings Bryan

I do believe we choose our own destiny. Sure, there are forces that are beyond our control, but for the most part, our choices determine the path our life takes. Go to college right out of high school or take a year off to travel the world? The rest of your life will be affected by that choice. Get married, buy a house, and settle down in your mid-20s? Or stay single, save a bundle, and live in a foreign country for a few years? Your choices form your life.

Today I will make wise choices, knowing each one may affect the goals and dreams I have for my life.

251

Loving Those Changes

"When you're finished changing, you're finished."
Benjamin Franklin

I have accumulated more than 100 photo albums over the course of my life, from the paint-by-number one that I made in grade school to the latest and greatest pictures of my grandkids and various travel activities. Flipping through these albums shows me that I have changed greatly in looks, size, demeanor, experience, and attitude over the years. I hope I'm growing older gracefully. I've learned that I can't control the wrinkles or the sags, but I can grow wiser and kinder. I don't ever want to finish changing; we are all works in progress.

Today I will not focus on my age spots or latest wrinkles. Instead I will seek out a new adventure or opportunity for growth.

Getting There Is Half the Fun

*"We may run, walk, stumble, drive, or fly, but let
us never lose sight of the reason for the journey
or miss a chance to see a rainbow on the way."*

Anonymous

*D*id you ever travel with someone who was
determined to get from point A to point B
the fastest way possible? They don't want to veer
off the road even five miles to see Mount Rushmore,
Lake Tahoe, or the Grand Canyon. I do understand
the need sometimes for trying to get somewhere
in the shortest amount of time possible. But when
we're traveling just to see the sights, perhaps we
can loosen up with books that can entice even the
most reluctant traveler to stop and smell the roses.
The same philosophy can apply to our everyday
lives; instead of just going from home to work and
back each day, we need to take some detours to
refresh our spirits and enlarge our hearts.

**Today I will deviate from my typical existence in
some way. Perhaps I will talk my friend into trying
a new restaurant or recipe with me.**

Resolve to Succeed

"Always bear in mind that your own resolution to succeed is more important than any one thing."

Abraham Lincoln

The first step toward anything is to resolve to do it. If our resolve is firm, nothing can stop us. Let's say your dream has always been to become a nurse so you could travel the world and help those in need. Making your dream come true will make all the classes and studying worth it. If you resolve to do it, you will do whatever it takes to make your dream come true.

Today I will ponder my goals and dreams, and I will resolve to make one of them come true.

The Artist Within

"I dream a lot. I do more painting when I'm not painting. It's in the subconscious."

Andrew Wyeth

When we use our natural talents, we are "working" all the time, but it does not feel like work—we are just doing what comes naturally to us. This is the best way to live—to spend all of our time perfecting creative works of love. If you could spend all of your time doing just one thing, what would you choose?

I will spend at least part of today doing something I love to do.

The Power of Learning

"Education, clear and simple, is power."

Hill Harper

The more we know about the world, the more power we have. Knowledge makes us useful—it can even make us indispensable. For example, if we are one of the few people with significant historical, economic, scientific, or engineering knowledge and understanding, others will look to us for help and guidance. There are all different types of knowledge. Some people learn by experience, others by schooling. Whatever kind of knowledge you have, use and expand upon it.

Today I will expand my mind. I will pick a topic of interest and research it at the library or on the Internet.

Simple Pleasures

"Teach us delight in simple things."
Rudyard Kipling

It's the complicated things in life that make us spin out of control, lose our ability to think clearly, and snap at our loved ones. The complicated things include work, household responsibilities, social commitments, and leisure activities. We must remember that our basic needs are simple, and life is full of simple pleasures: a few minutes to marvel at a blue sky; a quiet afternoon at the library; the enjoyment of a porch swing on a crisp autumn morning. Simple things bring significant delight to our lives.

Today I will enjoy simple pleasures. Perhaps I will stop by a senior living facility and play cards with some of the residents.

Learn, Baby, Learn

*"You cannot teach a man anything.
You can only help him discover it himself."*

Galileo

I teach writing, and I always tell my students good writing cannot be taught—it can only be learned. Two things are necessary in the teacher-student relationship: The teacher has to know the topic, and the student has to be open to learning. If either of these elements is off, the exercise is futile. People are not actually blank slates; they have innate propensities. We cannot just fill another person up with whatever knowledge we feel they need. But under the right circumstances, the butterfly will emerge and fly off on its own.

Today I will be open to learning something new.

Smiling Over the Hurt

"Optimism is the madness of maintaining that everything is right when it is wrong."

Voltaire

A positive outlook is important, but this doesn't mean we should live in a fantasy world and ignore all problems. It just means we don't let the "wrong" things in life lead us to despair. Every community has problems, and they can be extremely disheartening. Take violence, for instance. It is a deplorable thing to be afraid to go out in your community because it is held hostage by violence. A person living in a fantasy world cannot handle the problem and will pretend not to notice it. A despairing person will claim that the problem has destroyed the community. An optimist will look at the community and say yes, violence is a significant problem, but our community can come together and eradicate this problem. Start attending community meetings. Start talking to your neighbors, and work with and help each other. Even when everything seems wrong, an optimist knows that all is not lost.

Today I will be a realist *and* an optimist.

September 4

Learning the Hard Way

"Mistakes are their own instructors."

Horace

An art curator in New York commissioned 400 artists, including my daughter Jeanne, to each make a painting that measured exactly two feet by two feet. He wanted to hang the paintings in a perfect grid formation in a large gallery. The show would be titled *Size Matters*.

After Jeanne completed her watercolor, she went to a special archival artists store and purchased a scalpel to cut her painting. Gingerly placing her steel ruler along the sides of the painting, she sliced through the heavy paper. Surprised at her dexterity, she carefully measured out 24 inches on each side of the painting, turned it twice again, and made two more cuts along the pencil line she'd drawn.

Wow! I'm really good at this! Jeanne thought to herself. Totally relaxed, Jeanne felt her chest puff up with arrogance and pride in her work.

She turned the painting to make the final cut. Slice. The instant the scalpel left the paper, Jeanne realized she'd cut on the wrong side of the ruler, slicing off an inch-and-a-half too much of her precious painting.

"Mom," she told me later, "It was the minute I felt that cocky arrogance that I made the disastrous mistake!"

Jeanne salvaged the painting by applying adhesive to both pieces and attaching muslin to the back. I am sure some people who saw Jeanne's creation in that art show noticed the thin line where the painting had been cut and glued. Perhaps some of them even thought it was the artist's humorous way of saying that size does matter.

Jeanne's struggle reminded me that once a mistake has been made, it doesn't pay to fret—it pays to fix it the best way you know how.

Today I will not fret over any mistakes. I will remind myself that they are opportunities for learning, and I will fix them as best I can.

Eyes Wide Open

"Discovery consists of seeing what everybody has seen and thinking what nobody has thought."

Albert Szent-Györgyi

Think about important historical discoveries. Most of them were not inventions—they were the result of patiently studying something for a significant amount of time and coming to a conclusion that we now take for granted. Albert Szent-Györgyi, for example (the source of the above quote) studied vitamin C for years. He played a large role in comprehending the vitamin's properties and significance. Now, of course, we all know the importance of ingesting enough of this vitamin. The above quote can apply to the arts as well. Most great works of art do not depict amazing things; they just depict things from a perspective that makes them stand out. Think about Monet's haystacks. What could be more ordinary than a haystack? Yet Monet made them glorious.

Today I will make an effort to take a new look at seemingly mundane things.

Metamorphosis

*"We grow neither better nor worse as we
get old, but more like ourselves."*

May Lamberton Becker

The above quote is a simple fact, but it is one
that is easy to lose sight of. Sometimes we
do not feel like ourselves, and this is a disarming
feeling. We usually feel this way during times
of great change, however, and if we are patient,
we will soon feel more like ourselves than ever.
Every year we grow wiser and make progress into
becoming the individuals we are destined to be. At
the end of our lives, we are the wise product of a
lifetime of experiences, and we are sublime.

**Today I will face each experience with patience
and courage, keeping in mind that my character is
forever undergoing refinement.**

September 7

So Much to Learn

"He who knows best knows how little he knows."
Thomas Jefferson

The older I get, the more I realize how little I know. Every day I come across at least one topic I know nothing about, and that topic opens up another topic, which opens up another topic, and on and on. It can be overwhelming, but if we keep in mind that there will always be something more to learn, we can see the beauty of it. Learning is invigorating—without so many opportunities to learn, life would be static and dull.

Today I will endeavor to learn about one new topic. If I do this every day for the next year, I will be 365-things smarter in one year. Just one new thing a day—I can handle that.

Taking Stock of Our Assets

"The greatest good you can do for another is not just share your riches, but reveal to them their own."

Benjamin Disraeli

Sometimes it is hard to recognize our own talents. We may feel unsure, or we may be afraid that we will overestimate our strengths. That is when it is good to rely on the judgment of trusted associates and peers. They are the ones who can accurately gauge where our strengths and talents lie. We can do this for others as well.

Today if I notice a loved one or associate excelling at a task or endeavor, I will be sure to offer a compliment.

The Joy of a Good Harness

*"I'm not afraid of storms,
for I'm learning how to sail my ship."*

Louisa May Alcott

*I*magine being alone in a small sailboat on an open sea in the middle of a savage storm. A little scary, huh? Life is like that sometimes, though. It sucks us into a vortex so big and powerful we're sure the next destination is Oz and all we can do is hold on for dear life. Learning how to sail our ships means learning how to balance. Unknown balances with experience, and reckless balances with safety. We can have fun plunging into the unknown as long as we take precautions or at least do it with someone who knows how to handle any crisis that might come along.

Today I will feel confident, no matter what circumstances I face. I know I am prepared and can handle anything that comes along.

Banishing Fear with a Little Knowledge

"Nothing in life is to be feared.
It is only to be understood."

Marie Curie

What do you fear? Many people fear spiders, snakes, or ghosts. Others fear job loss. Still others fear illness, violence, or death. If we learn all we can about each of our fears, we'll begin to understand them and perhaps even gain a greater appreciation for the object of our fear. Watching a documentary on tornadoes, for instance, helps us learn when and where tornadoes are most likely to occur. The more we learn, the more prepared and self-assured we can be.

Today, I will work toward conquering one fear by researching it on the Internet.

September 11

Through the Desert

*"Hold no man responsible for
what he says in his grief."*
The Talmud

What thoughts go through our minds when we are grieving? *I'll never get over this. I cannot take this.* These are cries of desperation and despair. An old Jewish saying about behavior during grief was "he tore his garments." I used to think this saying was very odd, but how descriptive! When we are blindsided by grief, we do want to just rip something to shreds; we are not in our right minds. Luckily, our loved ones understand this because most of them have been through it. It takes time to move past what has occurred and make peace with it.

Today if I encounter someone who seems sad or troubled, I will be understanding.

Finding Answers in All the Right Places

"The greatest compliment that was ever paid me was when one asked me what I thought, and attended to my answer."

Henry David Thoreau

We have all had the dreaded experience of being asked our opinion and begun our answer, only to quickly notice the asker's vacant eyes and realize his or her mind is a million miles away. This experience leaves us with an empty, pointless feeling. Why bother to ask a person's opinion if you're not even going to have the courtesy to listen to the answer?

If I come across a perplexing problem today, I will think of a loved one who might have some advice. Once I have voiced my question, I will do nothing but listen attentively to the answer.

September 13

Doing What We Do Best

"Genius without education is like silver in the mine."
Benjamin Franklin

We're all born with a talent to do something amazing. One purpose of education is to help us discover that talent and make good use of it. We have to pull it out of the depths of our being, and then education will help us refine it and make it work. Only then will our lives sizzle with purpose and creativity.

Today I will read an article, watch a documentary, or sign up for a lecture or class. There's always more to learn, and I want to keep my talents from getting rusty.

Sock It to Me

"Slang is a language that rolls up its sleeves,
spits on its hands and goes to work."

Carl Sandburg

There are times for fancy language, and there are times to settle in and do the work that needs to be done. As we're working, we generally are not worried about appearances—we're focusing on completing the job at hand. When the job is near completion, there will be time for refinement.

Today I will focus on getting things done.

September 15

Philosophy of Life

*"An American Religion: Work, play, breathe,
bathe, study, live, laugh, and love."*

Elbert Hubbard

*E*lbert Hubbard was an American writer.
On May 1, 1915, he and his wife boarded
the *Lusitania* in New York City. A week later, the
ship was torpedoed. During the panic immediately
following the impact, one of the other passengers
asked the couple what they were going to do.
Hubbard smiled and said, "There does not seem to
be anything to do." And with that he and his wife
waited calmly for their fate. They ended up going
down with the ship. I wonder—could we accept our
impending deaths so matter-of-factly? Perhaps we
could if we lived full, simple lives, working, playing,
breathing, bathing, studying, living, laughing, and
loving.

**Today I will make a point to incorporate all eight
of the above activities into my life.**

Ask Away

"Judge people by their questions
rather than by their answers."

Voltaire

*O*ur questions reveal our interests; they are topics we initiate, while our answers are about topics initiated by others. What kinds of questions do you tend to ask? Think of the questions you've recently asked yourself, the ones you've posed to associates or loved ones, and those you've typed into a search engine. They reveal what you care about, what you hold dear. Obviously a mix of questions is healthy, but it is good if the majority of our questions deal with substantial rather than frivolous concerns. Do we want to know about a celebrity's dirty laundry, or would we prefer to hear about causes they support? Do we want to know how much money a person makes or what kind of car they drive, or do we want to know about their loved ones and their hobbies?

**Today I will be mindful when posing questions.
I will be sure they reveal my true concerns.**

Strength of Purpose

"It is wonderful what strength of purpose and boldness and energy of will are roused by the assurance that we are doing our duty."

Sir Walter Scott

What is our duty, our calling in this world? This is usually found only after great reflection. Sometimes it takes years to determine our true calling. Some of us have a talent for sharing knowledge and passing on information, and we come to the realization that our calling is to teach. Others may realize they have compassion, strong stomachs, and a knack for science, and they go on to work in the medical field. Still others feel most invigorated by creativity and go into the arts. Finding our true calling is paramount because this way, we feel assured and fulfilled every day. If we feel we are spending each day toiling uselessly, time drags on and our existence lacks meaning.

Today I will set aside some time to ponder what my duty or calling in this world might be. If I find this overwhelming, I will simply choose a duty for today, and I will work at accomplishing it.

Jump Out of the Box

"Think left and think right and think low and think high. Oh, the things you can think up if only you try!"

Theodor Seuss Geisel

Sometimes it's good to let your mind wander. Sure, there are times when we must be focused on a task, but we also need to set aside time to just be imaginative. Otherwise we may find ourselves stuck in the same uninspired routine day after day. The ideal time for letting our minds wander is while traveling to a new place. Any inspiration you get can only benefit your standard routine.

Today I will travel to a new place or rediscover an old haunt. I will approach everything with an open mind, and I will feel invigorated.

September 19

Perfection

"I am careful not to confuse excellence with perfection. Excellence, I can reach for, perfection is God's business."

Michael J. Fox

$\mathcal{E}$xcellence is a colorful quilt lovingly stitched by hand. Perfection is a sunset that mingles stunning colors of red, orange, yellow, blue, and turquoise among clouds of breathtaking shapes. Excellence is a well-crafted thesis. Perfection is a blue ocean with soft waves that lap against a majestic shoreline composed of fine white sand. Perfection is breathtaking, but excellence is gratifying in its own right, as it is achieved through hard, steady work.

Today I will work with excellence as my goal.

September 20

School Daze

"In youth we learn; in age we understand."

Marie Ebner-Eschenbach

As a child, I wasn't always crazy about waiting for the school bus on those cold winter mornings. I would stand there, freezing in the northern Illinois wind and snow. And often it was a frustrating experience to sit in those classrooms, especially when there were 50 kids in the class and one-on-one attention was unheard of. But thank goodness I stuck with it. I went to school, sat still, studied, memorized, recited, wrote, and yes, I learned. Now, decades later, I understand why I had to stand in the cold and wait for the bus to take me to that cramped classroom.

Today I will embrace every opportunity to learn something new.

September 21

I'm All Ears

*"If we were supposed to talk more than we listen,
we would have two mouths and one ear."*

Mark Twain

During a slightly rough patch in my ever-growing relationship with the love of my life, we both felt a little pressure from each other about expectations. We came to the conclusion that we both needed to listen more and talk less. We also decided to spill the beans each evening before bedtime to clear the air and say what's on our minds. We listen to each other and really try to put ourselves in the other's shoes. Spilling the beans has worked to help us both be better listeners... and better friends.

Today I will endeavor to listen more than I talk.

Think Before You Speak

"If A is success in life, then A equals x plus y plus z. Work is x; y is play; and z is keeping your mouth shut."

Albert Einstein

Our mouths have a capacity to get us into *deep* trouble, don't they? If we have a hard time keeping secrets, people lose trust in us. Or, if we tend to rant when we're upset, we may say things we wouldn't normally think, let alone say out loud. There are many times in life when it's better to keep our mouths shut.

Today I will work on thinking before I speak, and I will keep my mouth shut at the appropriate times.

Come to Dinner

"All great change in America begins at the dinner table."

Ronald Reagan

Many family counselors stress the importance of family meals. It makes sense when you think about it—having children get used to sharing around a table fosters discussion and relationships. It is a regular time to share, feel heard, and enjoy each other's company. Turn off the TV, the computer, the video games, the cell phones, and all other distractions. It's dinnertime—all hands on deck.

Today I will set the table, cook something up, and invite a friend or loved one to share a meal and some conversation with me. Soup's on!

Time in a Bottle

*"You will never find time for anything.
If you want time you must make it."*

Charles Buxton

How many times have you said to yourself, "I wish I had time for that"? If it is something you sincerely long to do, make plans to do it. Otherwise, it is easy to let your daily routine get in the way. Do you long to get into a good exercise routine but find it difficult to "find the time"? Perhaps get up a little earlier each day and take a morning walk or fit in a walk during your lunch hour. Before you know it, it will be as routine as brushing your teeth.

If I find myself wishing I had time to do something today, I will look through my calendar and carve out time for it.

September 25

The Brotherhood of Work

*"Anybody can sympathize with the sufferings
of a friend, but it requires a very fine nature
to sympathize with a friend's success."*

Oscar Wilde

When a friend achieves sudden success, it's tempting to feel left in the dust. Who wants to be the brooding, selfish person trying to hold a loved one back, though? Plus, who knows what's around the corner for us? Perhaps through our friend's newfound success we'll meet new people or encounter new opportunities as well. Be the first to offer congratulations—it's what you would want from your friend, and you will never regret it. We all have times to shine and moments to be cheerleaders. Our next time to shine will come.

Today if something good happens to an associate or a loved one, I will be the first to congratulate them on a job well done.

What Is Success, Anyway?

"Try not to become a man of success.
Rather become a man of value."

Albert Einstein

*M*any people can be considered successful, can't they? Some shady lawyers make as much or more money than the lawyers who work for years to reverse a ruling against the wrongfully accused. If you measure success by the type of car you drive or the house you are able to afford, both individuals are successful. Only one is a person of value, however. The real heroes of our world are the soldiers, firefighters, police officers, businesspeople, teachers, parents, and others who safeguard or improve our communities every day.

Today I will think about my work and whether or not it is of value. If it is not, I will consider a career change or devote more time to volunteering in my community.

Moving On

"They say that time changes things, but you actually have to change them yourself."

Andy Warhol

In 2006, my sister's only son was killed tragically in a plane crash. An 18-year-old aviation student, he was piloting the plane at the time of the crash. Losing a child is almost more than one can bear. Time did not ease this loss, so my sister had to muster the strength to change things herself. She thought a change of scenery might help, so she and her husband moved to a warmer, sunnier climate and downsized their home. They survived and have found renewed happiness.

If anything brings me down today, I will try to figure out a way to change things myself.

September 28

Breathe Deeply

"Encouragement is the oxygen of the soul."
George M. Adams

When my son Michael made plans to attend a men's retreat at his church, loved ones were asked to write letters of encouragement for the men to read during the weekend. I wrote two pages, single-spaced, and I could have kept going for many more pages. I wanted Michael to feel that whoosh of fresh oxygen sweep through his soul as he read my letter. I wanted him to feel encouraged.

Today if I notice an associate or loved one getting discouraged, I will offer encouragement.

September 29

Make Use of Your Talents

*"Be faithful to that which exists nowhere but in
yourself and thus make yourself indispensable."*
André Gide

truly believe that each of us has at least one
special talent. It is up to us to discover it and
put it to use. Once those around us notice our
talent, we become an indispensable part of our
community. Wouldn't the world be an amazingly
beautiful place if we all reached our full potential?

**Today I will reflect upon my specific talents and
make sure I am putting them to use.**

Stepping Up to the Plate

*"It is hard to fail; but it is worse
never to have tried to succeed."*

Theodore Roosevelt

ailure hurts; it is hard to admit, and it sometimes embarrasses us. We all have been touched by failure, though, haven't we? And what happens after failure? We get up, dust ourselves off, and begin anew. Failure is a deflating feeling, but the worst feeling of all is coming to the end of our time on this earth and realizing we never went after our dreams because we were too afraid to take any chances—we were too afraid of failure. Pursue your dreams. You may fail; if you do, you will begin again. And if you succeed—well, can you imagine the invigorating feeling? It is surely among the best feelings we can ever have.

Today I will step up to the plate and do something to move my goals forward.

Stepping Out of Ourselves

"Daring ideas are like chessmen moved forward.
They may be beaten, but they may
start a winning game."

Johann Wolfgang von Goethe

We can think of life as a game, can't we? We either take daring chances, or we play it safe. Why not be daring? We only live once. Let's say you adore flowers and your dream is to open your own flower shop. Why not save up and try to get there? Maybe it will turn into a flourishing business and people in the neighborhood will clamor to have you as their florist for every momentous occasion. Sure, your move may end in defeat, but if you give it your all, the odds are in your favor.

Today I choose to be daring. I will move forward with the plan that I have been putting off.

A Symphony of Drummers

"If a man does not keep pace with his companions, perhaps it is because he hears a different drummer. Let him step to the music he hears, however measured and far away."

Henry David Thoreau

My friends are varied and original, and I love this about them. One couple lives in the mountains and doesn't get too upset when one of their chickens wanders into the house. Another friend lives in a small New York apartment on the 18th floor and loves every minute of the Manhattan hubbub. I choose a quiet life in a condo near the water. Each of us marches to a different drummer, but we contribute to the magnificent symphony that is our world.

Today I will invite my friend to come visit me. Maybe next year I'll visit her and experience city life for a few days.

289

October 3

Keep at It

"It's always too early to quit."
Norman Vincent Peale

Are there times in your life when you have quit? Most of us have quit at something, and most of us have ended up regretting it. Perhaps you endeavored to start a consistent workout routine but quit after a few sessions because it was "too hard." Most worthy endeavors are difficult; they get easier with time, however, and the benefits we reap in the end are certainly worth it. If you find yourself getting discouraged, take stock of your plan and maybe ease up on yourself a bit, but don't quit. Quitting isn't an option.

If I am tempted to quit something today, I will take some deep breaths and begin again.

The Joy of Learning

*"With courage you can stay with something
long enough to succeed at it."*

Earl Nightingale

*F*ew things come to us naturally. Take skiing,
for instance: Does anyone ski effortlessly down
the hill on his or her first attempt? Perhaps, but
surely this is a rare occurrence. Most of us fall all
over the place before we are steady on skis. But the
joy such an activity can bring us is well worth all
the imperfect runs.

**If I am daunted by anything today, I will endeavor
to stick with it until I am proficient.**

Playing It Safe

*"Don't think there are no crocodiles
because the water is calm."*

Anonymous

/ find alligators fascinating. I will bike five miles each way to a park in my area to observe the gators that live there. Once, soon after I moved to Florida, I was riding my bike on the narrow path around the perimeter of that park. I glimpsed a six-foot-long gator sunning itself along the lake. I jumped off my bike, grabbed my camera, and quietly moved closer to get a good shot.

At one point, I was five feet from the amazing creature. As I took another step, the gator slowly moved toward the water, which rippled as the gator inched its way in. I stepped closer. Just as I lifted my camera, I heard a loud grunting sound, and then the gator turned and slapped the water with its tail. It was telling me to back off! I jumped on my bike and never looked back.

I learned later that an alligator can run as fast as a horse. I realized I'd better keep my distance, especially during mating season. I reflected upon my new life in Florida and all the things I had to learn to respect. The Florida sun is another good example; it too can be a killer. I now apply sunscreen liberally before venturing out.

Another thing I need to learn to respect is my diet. There are so many restaurants and early-bird specials down here, it would be easy to eat out three or four times a week. But I need to avoid the rich, fatty foods that are the staples at most restaurants.

Yes, those gators have taught me a lot about respecting others as well as myself. The water may seem calm, but danger lurks—especially at the all-you-can-eat Chinese buffet.

Today I will be on my guard. I will be ready for whatever comes my way.

October 6

Star Light, Star Bright

*"The stars speak of man's insignificance
in the long eternity of time."*

Edwin Way Teale

When we glimpse a starry sky, most of us just gaze in wonder at the sight. We do this because it is truly beautiful, but the sight also tends to remind us of the vastness of the universe. We feel very small at these times, but this is oddly reassuring and refreshing. The spectacular view frees our mind from our day-to-day troubles; as we see how small we are, we see how our troubles are even smaller in the grand scheme of things.

If anything starts to bring me down today, I will reflect on whether or not it is a significant problem. Most irritants really are small problems if we take a step back.

Living Life to the Max

"You cannot learn to skate without being ridiculous. The ice of life is slippery."

George Bernard Shaw

*L*ife is not easy, and if we make a habit of trying new things, life gets even harder and more complicated. But what is the alternative? To stay completely safe, we would have to remain home all the time. If we take this route, we never go anywhere or do anything. What kind of life is that? Make peace with being ridiculous at times—it is part of life. When my life is over, I want to be splattered with mud from head to toe as I kick that last ball through the goalposts. I want to know and feel like I've been there, and done that. I want to have slipped and slid across every stretch of our adventure-filled planet.

If I make a mistake today, I will not let it get me down. I will keep plowing through and start planning my next adventure.

October 8

Dare to Be Great

"Be not afraid of greatness: Some are born great, some achieve greatness, and some have greatness thrust upon them."

William Shakespeare

Greatness can be daunting, for with greatness comes great responsibility. Take those who are born great—Prince William and Prince Harry, for instance. They did not ask to be born into the limelight, but they roll with it gracefully the majority of the time. Most of us can only achieve greatness on our own. If we seem to have great talent, we must go for it—we should not be afraid. What is there to lose? Maybe we will not actually achieve greatness, but we will know we made the most of our talents and capabilities. And if we find ourselves with greatness thrust upon us—perhaps by having an opportunity to be a hero during a crisis—well, we certainly must not shrink from that. We must take a deep breath, have courage, and seize the opportunity before us. Certainly we have something to offer in such a dire circumstance.

If an opportunity presents itself today, I will seize it and not be afraid.

Funny Bones

*"You don't stop laughing because you grow old;
you grow old because you stop laughing."*

Michael Pritchard

Growing old is tough. Your joints start to creak, your blood pressure likely inches up, and it seems like you need the TV volume higher every day. Have you noticed, though, how some older people are still smiling through it all, while others appear miserable? Sure, some people have been dealt some tough breaks, but attitude makes a difference as well. If we keep laughing and don't despair over our troubles, we can feel decades younger than our actual age. Keep smiling—it's a bona fide face-lift.

I will make sure to fit some laughter into my day today. If I don't find myself laughing during my normal routine, I will read a humorous article or watch a funny show before I hit the sack.

297

Take That First Step

"All know the way; few actually walk it."
Bodhidharma

We all instinctively know what life takes, don't we? It generally takes determination and hard work. Often, we hesitate committing ourselves to the work before us because we feel lazy or scared. We may feel relatively content with the way things are, so we are lazy about going after something better. Or we are scared that we might fail, or that it will be a lot of work without as much reward as we would like. It is easier to just let time go by, but we must take that first step and conquer the roadblocks we have set before ourselves. It is more honorable and rewarding to do what we know we should be doing. Those who are determined to realize their dreams see the way as a stimulating, beautiful, challenging adventure.

I will not give in to laziness or fear today. I know what needs to be done, and I will do it.

Mother Nature Rules

"No matter how rich you become, how famous or powerful, when you die the size of your funeral will still pretty much depend on the weather."

Michael Pritchard

We make big plans, but Mother Nature has her way in the end, doesn't she? Let's say you live in the Midwest and plan a winter getaway to Florida. You make plans to fly out on February 2. If a blizzard blows in that morning, all your planning may well be for naught. Sometimes—even in this modern world of ours—it really is impossible to get to our destination in time. Make big plans, but be ready to make peace with whatever happens.

Today I will be ready to accept things that are beyond my control.

Happy Birthday

*"Write it on your heart that every day
is the best day in the year."*

Ralph Waldo Emerson

October 12 is my birthday. For me and for a half dozen other people I know who were born on Columbus Day, this really is the best day of the year. Unlike some people who are inching their way into their middle or late years and prefer to have their birthdays ignored, I look forward to my birthday as it gets closer. I like looking back over a mostly happy year and enjoy the heck out of my big day, which is generally filled with surprises and time spent with loved ones. I also enjoy looking forward to all my tomorrows, no matter how old I get. Every day truly should be the best day of the year because it is the day that is before us, with all of its possibilities. What are you going to do today?

I will make the most of the day that is before me. Perhaps I will make plans to visit a place I've only heard about.

Compliments Lead to Confidence

"You're braver than you believe, and stronger than you seem, and smarter than you think."

Christopher Robin

It is nice to be considered brave, strong, and smart—it makes us feel good and capable. Compliments lead to confidence, and confidence can get us anywhere. Take the chef who felt capable of opening his own restaurant because loved ones had raved about his cooking expertise. The residents of the chef's community are grateful for a wonderful new restaurant, and they are grateful to the people who encouraged the chef to open it.

Today I will find a reason to compliment someone.

Focus on Hope

"Hope is like the sun, which, as we journey towards it, casts the shadow of our burden behind us."

Samuel Smiles

Hope can get us through any rough spots in our lives. Let's say we are facing a layoff, or a breakup, or the loss of a loved one. We get through these circumstances by focusing on hope and reminding ourselves that just as good times do not last, bad times do not either. We get out of a funk by distracting ourselves and looking ahead to new things. With time, sure enough, our burdens are behind us.

Today I will have hope for the future.

Playing Fair

*"Victory goes to the player who makes
the next-to-last mistake."*

Savielly Grigorievitch Tartakower

*M*ost competitions are not blowouts, and sometimes the team way ahead near the beginning of the game loses steam by the end. Other competitions are like fierce battles, with each team gaining ground on each turn. A good philosophy is to just be steady and keep competing because you never know what might happen. Perhaps your opponents will lose *their* heads, and the game will simply fall into your lap.

Today I will pick a favorite game and ask a friend to play with me. I won't quit before the game is over, and if I lose, I won't pout for an hour afterward.

October 16

Sticking Your Neck Out

*"Behold the turtle. He makes progress
only when he sticks his neck out."*

James Bryant Conant

The turtle has one of the sturdiest coats of armor in all of the animal kingdom. Those hard shells protect them from stronger, faster animals. It would be easy for the turtle to keep its head buried in that tough shell and stay protected all its life. But instead, it waits for its moment, then sticks its head out, explores what's around it, and makes its way. We humans have to expose ourselves to risk every day or we'll never get anywhere either. But the rewarding experiences are well worth the risks.

Today I will step out into the world with no fear.

Make Peace with the Process

*"I have not failed. I've just found
10,000 ways that won't work."*

Thomas Alva Edison

*E*dison sure was an optimist, wasn't he? He never focused on failure—just on researching possibilities. That's a good attitude for any of us. When you think about the universe, the possibilities are endless. Endless possibilities entail endless possibilities for failure as well as success. The only way we can make progress is by experimentation, and failure goes hand in hand with experimentation. But we must not let failure discourage us—it is simply part of the process.

Today I will experiment with something new, and I will not get discouraged if things go awry.

October 18

Glory Be

"Glory is fleeting, but obscurity is forever."
Napoléon Bonaparte

*G*lory certainly is fleeting, especially in our hectic modern world. Most of us have trouble remembering this morning's top stories, much less stories from weeks past. But it is better to have some goal in sight than to do nothing and leave no mark at all. We must find and claim our destiny, whether we play a major or supporting role in world events.

Today I will make progress at leaving my mark on the world.

Power Among Us

"If there is a faith that can move mountains, it is faith in your own power."

Marie Ebner von Eschenbach

The first step toward making something happen is believing that it can, in fact, happen. Take the famous example of the mother who was able to lift a car to free her trapped child. An unbelievable feat, right? So what explains it? Sheer will on behalf of the mother (and a little adrenaline thrown in for good measure). This is an extreme example, but it illustrates the fact that nearly anything can happen. Nothing should hold us back.

Today I will believe in myself as I pursue my dreams.

October 20

Make a Day of Happy

"Reflect on your present blessings, of which every man has many; not on your past misfortunes, of which all men have some."
Charles Dickens

It's easy to let our past misfortunes continue to affect our lives. Perhaps our childhood was not picture perfect. But whose was? Even the most blessed individuals in the world had significant obstacles to overcome—that is part of growing up.

Maybe our parents failed us in some way. As we age, it is important to realize that even though we idealized our parents when we were young, they are imperfect human beings just like the rest of us. We must accept this, find a way to forgive them, and move on.

Nothing can be done about our various past misfortunes; we must leave them in the past. Don't give them the power to hold you back now or in the future. This is the present, and we all have numerous specific blessings if we take the time to appreciate them.

What are you thankful for right now? Maybe you have a terrific family or friends who are like the most supportive family anyone could ever want. Maybe you have a fantastic job, your dream house, a wonderful pet, or the means to travel the world. Focus on the here and now—what you can work with—and leave the past where it belongs.

Right now I will think of three things I am thankful for. If I begin to feel down later today, I will remind myself of these specific blessings.

October 21

Books, the Perfect Companions

*"A good book is the best of friends,
the same today and forever."*

Martin Fraquhar Tupper

Think about the greatest books you've ever read. It is amazing how a book really can feel like a good friend. If the writer is brilliant with character development, we feel we know the characters as well as we know our closest friends. A book can take us to places we've only dreamed of. Sometimes it feels as though a good book gives us what we need, exactly when we need it. Such a work of art reaches into the depths of our being and makes us see the world from a new, refreshing perspective. A good book challenges us and changes us—we are never quite the same after having read it.

Today I will browse the books at a bookstore, library, or online. Perhaps one will catch my eye and become my new favorite.

The Gist of Joy

"Joy is a net of love."

Mother Teresa

Joy is contagious. If you endeavor to remain joyful, whatever circumstances you face each day, you are acting in a loving way toward those around you. It is hard to fathom the number of people who can be touched by one joyful person. If you ride the bus each day and smile when you catch the eyes of other passengers, it is hard for them not to smile back or at least notice the joy that emanates from you. Perhaps your joy will help them feel a little more joyful throughout the day.

Today I choose to be happy and spread the joy.

October 23

Never Too Old to Learn Something New

"Try to learn something about everything and everything about something."

Thomas Henry Huxley

There's so much information in this world of ours that it is impossible for any of us to know everything. We can, however, begin by learning everything about our one area of expertise, then endeavor to learn at least a little about everything else. This way, we know enough to be successful and to be able to carry on a conversation with anyone we might meet. I've studied, read, asked questions, traveled to 15 different countries, and written letters, stories, articles, and books. I've learned, shared, and experienced something about many things, and I am grateful to still be doing all of these things.

Today I will refresh my knowledge about my area of expertise by rereading something instructive, and I will expand my horizons in some way. Perhaps I'll take a look at my library's event listings and make plans to attend a session or two.

Get Out There

"Man is born to live, not to prepare for life."
Boris Pasternak

*S*tudy certainly prepares us for life, but experience must follow soon after study, shouldn't it? The experience phase must not be delayed too long. Studying feels empty after a certain point. It is like watching a fabulous travel or cooking show—we are enticed, but then we want the experience for ourselves. Prepare well enough, then get out there and live.

Today I will make sure I am prepared, but I will focus on living.

Try It Again

"It is difficulties that show what men are."
Epictetus

How did you handle the most difficult time in your life? You could have handled it differently, right? Either you handled it with strength and courage when you could have dodged it, or you dodged it when you could have exhibited strength of character. Think of the scene in *Les Misérables* when Jean Valjean had a chance to let an innocent man be held in his place. Freedom was tempting, but Jean Valjean was too noble to take it at such a price.

Today I will face my difficulties with courage.

Make the Most of Each Minute

*"In the end, it's not the years in your life
that count. It's the life in your years."*

Abraham Lincoln

How do you begin each day? Do you start optimistically and full of life (after that first cup of coffee or tea, of course), or grumpily waiting for the next annoying thing to happen? Circumstances can seem to account for our outlook, but this is not true across the board, is it? Haven't we all noticed both miserable heiresses and happy-go-lucky toilers? Don't waste your days worrying or focusing on the imperfect aspects of life. Find joy where you can and make the most of each minute of every day. If we live this way, it won't matter if we live to be 35 or 105—we will have made the most of our time on this earth.

I am grateful for the day before me, and I will make the most of it.

Dreams to Change the World

"Those who dream by day are cognizant of many things which escape those who dream only by night."

Edgar Allan Poe

Some of us have jobs that do not lend themselves to daydreaming; we must be focused much of the time, but we still have the hours of the day that we devote to our own pursuits. Take time to dream during those times. If we let our minds wander only at night (when there's no rhyme or reason to the wandering), we become mere robots with no thoughts or ideas of our own.

Perhaps you take the train to work and have time to let your mind wander. Or perhaps you have time for yoga or meditation at night. Get yourself into a meditative posture and clear all thoughts from your brain. Now say to yourself, "One way I can make my life better is..." Or, "Is a friend or family member going through a rough patch right now? What can I do to help them out?" Or, "If I could change the world, I'd..." Let the daydreams begin.

Today I will daydream. Perhaps I will come up with a creative solution to a vexing problem.

The Power Is Out There

"There are no great limits to growth because there are no limits of human intelligence, imagination, and wonder."

Ronald Reagan

Before their experiments took off, the Wright brothers were probably considered a little crazy, right? Now, however, we take air travel for granted. Who knows, perhaps you live next door to the Wright brothers of today, or perhaps you have your own ongoing experiments. Human beings are an industrious bunch, and the opportunities are unlimited.

Today I will reflect upon the problems facing my community, and I will try to come up with some inventive solutions or ways to help.

Making It Work

"Fall down seven times, get up eight."

Japanese Proverb

Falling down is a deflating experience. It usually hurts a little, and it is sometimes embarrassing. But we get back up after each fall because our only other choice is to remain on the ground, and what's the use in that? While we are able to get back up, there's hope. If we can get up, that means we can likely take another step, and we can eventually make it to our destination.

If I fall today, I will get right back up. I will not let anything defeat me.

Work Is More Than a Four-Letter Word

"Opportunity is missed by most people because it is dressed in overalls and looks like work."

Thomas Alva Edison

Ideas come to each of us nearly every day, but often we write them off out of laziness. Perhaps we think someone else has probably already come up with a better product, or we are not really sure how to proceed, or we don't have the money to get started. There's always an excuse not to start something. Every worthwhile pursuit involves work, and often aspects of the job are boring or messy. Just get started—there will be time later to go back over your work and revise, revise, revise. Be a doer; it will set you apart, and who knows where it will lead. Take Edison's experiments—many of them were surely boring and repetitive, but they led to amazing things. Without his work on the lightbulb and phonograph, our electrified, recorded world of today would likely be very different.

Today I will work with gusto. Bring it on!

Guided Explosions

*"Anger is never without reason,
but seldom with a good one."*

Benjamin Franklin

A fit of anger is like a balloon that pops right in your face. First, you have a balloon (that would be you). Then you have a pump (something that ticks you off). Then you have hot air (you and the pump create this together—the pump sends the air your way, and you allow the air to build up inside you). If you don't do anything to diffuse the air, POP! You explode, scaring everyone in the immediate area. Nobody wants to see that.

When I feel anger welling up inside me, I will handle it constructively. If my anger is toward a person, I will talk things out. If it is of a more general kind, I will turn to yoga, my journal, or a hot bath.

Here They Come!

"I delight in others. I play with them and laugh with them and enjoy each moment. These are the pearls of life. They come one at a time."

Laurie Beth Jones

I feel lucky to live in Florida. Most people—especially those who live up north—love to come to Florida during the cold months. We call these visitors snowbirds. They start arriving in droves around the first of November, and the biggest rush comes right after the holidays. Things are pretty quiet down here for the other half of the year, but once the snowbirds start arriving, the fun begins: more dinners out with snowbird friends, and more parties, movies, art shows, and live theater events. We dance, laugh, sing, and eat out more than we should; we know these months will fly by, though, so we make the most of them while we can.

Today I will make plans for quality time spent with friends. Maybe I will organize a big night out at our favorite restaurant.

Making It Happen

"Let us not be content to wait and see what will happen, but give us the determination to make the right things happen."

Peter Marshall

Making the right things happen takes significant effort on our part. We have to sign petitions, choose which candidates to support, put up signs in our front yard, attend meetings, and exercise our right to vote. We cannot just sit back and hope everything will come out all right through others' efforts.

Today I will reflect upon the biggest problems in my community, and I will figure out a way to be part of at least one solution.

Brain Power

***"We should not only use the brains
we have, but all that we borrow."***

Woodrow Wilson

*A*ll those brainiacs who came before us
left us with untold numbers of facts,
systems, theories, and plans. The beauty of it is
that it's ours for the taking. All the information
past generations have gathered is just background
material for our own discoveries. So get crackin'.
Complete a masterpiece that *you* can leave behind.

**Today I will not hesitate to lean on past research to
propel my new ideas forward.**

Just a Number

"There is no old age. There is,
as there always was, just you."

Carol Matthau

Fretting about age is a pointless use of energy.
There are good and bad aspects to every
age. Each year we grow older, but we also grow
wiser—why not focus on the wise part? Sure, being
young is fun; everything is new and exciting, and
we feel capable of anything. This world of ours is
immense, though—there is always something new
and exciting, no matter how old we are. Do you feel
like your life has become routine and all the fun is
behind you? Nonsense. Start planning and saving
for a trip to a new destination or take up a new
hobby. Are you new to skiing, painting, writing, or
photography? Take a stab at something new and
feel young again.

**Today I will try something new, and I will expand
on the set of experiences that makes up my
wonderful life.**

The Whole Truth and Nothing But

"As scarce as truth is, the supply has always been in excess of the demand."

Josh Billings

Around election time, many of us ponder the fundamentals of our society. We review the basic issues that confront us, and we try to elect the best people to take us forward. In our modern world, it is easy to take a backseat and just assume things will continue to proceed as they should because we live in a free, civilized society. This is dangerous thinking, however. If we all took a backseat, who would safeguard the principles that have brought us to this point? We need to demand truth and excellence. Even if we ourselves are not capable of handling the various issues our government faces, surely we can choose the best candidates and entrust them with the top jobs.

Today I will do my research, and I will support the most capable and trustworthy candidates from my community.

November 6

The Music's in You

"There's no retirement for an artist, it's your way of living so there's no end to it."

Henry Moore

Artists squint at everything; they see the world in a whole different light. Drummers are also artists, and they can't get away from their calling either. You can spot a drummer by the constant tap-tap-tapping they do with everything within their reach—feet, fingers, straws, and silverware. Creative people feel creative all the time—it's part of their very being. They can't get away from it, and I imagine they don't want to.

Today I will nurture my creative side. Perhaps I will start a journal or sign up for a drawing class.

The Gumption of Assumption

"Begin challenging your own assumptions.
Your assumptions are your windows on
the world. Scrub them off every once in a
while, or the light won't come in."

Alan Alda

What's an assumption you made in the past that experience forced you to revise? Perhaps you grew up with the assumption that anyone who believed in God was stupid and judgmental. Later you got to know a religious person through working with him or her in close quarters, and you were shocked to realize the two of you actually had a lot in common. Or perhaps it was the other way around—you were the religious one and assumed any nonbeliever was evil or cruel. You got to know a nonbeliever, and you realized he or she was actually a lot like you. Experience is everything.

Today I will not assume anything—I will simply take each moment and interaction as it comes.

The Future Is Ours for the Making

"The best way to predict the future is to invent it."
Alan Kay

If you were to visit a palm reader or a psychic, what would you want them to tell you? That you are going to change the world or be part of an amazing love story? Why not start working on achieving those dreams today? If your dream is to change the world, how do you want to go about it? By joining the Peace Corps? Look into it today. Maybe your dream is to become a politician and take part in drafting the legislation that affects all of us. Look into running for a board or joining a committee in your area, and work your way up. If you are dreaming of a soul mate, just get out there and start meeting people. Join a club, say yes to every invitation you receive for the next month, or throw a party of your own. Just get out there. What are you waiting for?

Today I will start making my future happen.

The Joy of Learning

"There is no shame in not knowing…
the shame lies in not finding out."
Russian Proverb

I always loved teachers who began each semester by saying, "In this class, there are no dumb questions. Ask away." I am a curious person. If I don't know something, I'll ask the first person I see who might have the answer. These days, nearly every question can be answered on the Internet. Perhaps you shy away from all the discussions about health care because it seems overwhelming. Start researching it, and start having conversations. Or maybe the whole climate change controversy, or handgun legislation, or other contentious issues confuse you. Start figuring them out.

Today if a topic comes up that I am unfamiliar with, I will do a little research on it.

Practice, Practice, Practice

*"I have missed more than 9,000 shots in my career.
I have lost almost 300 games. On 26 occasions I have
been entrusted to take the game winning shot...
and I missed. I have failed over and over and over
again in my life. And that's precisely why I succeed."*

Michael Jordan

*F*ailures are simply practice. If you examine the lives of the most successful people throughout history, you will discover that before they achieved success, they experienced many failures. Failures strengthen us and spur us on. Once we have gotten right back up, we realize failure is no big deal. We are no longer afraid and focus instead on our next attempts. Failure makes future attempts stronger because we know what didn't work the last time. Experiencing failure pushes many of us to want success all the more.

Today I will not give up. I will try again and again, until I succeed.

The Face of Courage

"Courage is fear holding on a minute longer."

George S. Patton

The bravest among us feel fear—they just do not give in to it. They persist, because what is the other option? Give in? No—what kind of life is that? Better to be strong until the last breath.

Today I will send a letter to a soldier serving in a war zone. I will thank him or her for being a hero to all of us back home.

Sources of Light

*"There are two ways of spreading light;
to be the candle or the mirror that reflects it."*

Edith Wharton

Some of us are blessed with more obvious talents, but we all have something to offer. The candles of the world are the stars, and the mirrors are the supporting players. For instance, inventors are candles, and the people who get the word out about the invention are the mirrors. Both candles and mirrors have definite places in this world.

Today I will reflect on my talents, and I will endeavor to be a candle or a mirror.

Grabbing for Gusto

"Life is either a daring adventure or nothing. To keep our faces toward change and behave like free spirits in the presence of fate is strength undefeatable."

Helen Keller

If we take a step back from our daily routines, life really does seem like a daring adventure. We must grab it by the horns and relish every moment we have. We can read about a distant land—Italy, Egypt, or maybe Morocco. We can save up, learn the language, and take it all in. If we never experience adventures, life really is hours of nothing. Fear should not hold us back—bad things can happen, but they can happen in our living rooms. Step out, and try something new.

Today I will start planning a daring adventure.

November 14

Two Sides to Every Story

*"In seeking truth, you have to get
both sides of a story."*

Walter Cronkite

When we hear a story, it is good to make sure it is the whole story. This is a chief component of the best societies. Take the suspect who has been apprehended. Of course the police have reason to suspect the individual, but he is not wantonly punished. He is entitled to have his side of the story heard, and a jury will decide his fate. It is best for all involved if the truth prevails. True, it would be a terrible thing for a dangerous criminal to go free, but it would be equally terrible for an innocent man to lose his freedom.

Today I will be careful not to jump to conclusions.

A Friend Is as a Friend Does

"A friend is one who walks in when others walk out."
Walter Winchell

Think back to the hardest time in your life. Who stayed by your side, even when it was not easy to do? Those are your true friends. They know you inside and out, and they know that even if you made a mistake, that is not representative of who you really are. They focus on your most noble attributes and stand with you until the end.

Today I will call a close friend and invite her over for a cup of tea. I want to keep our bond strong.

Seeing Myself Through the Eyes of Others

"When you reread a classic you do not see more in the book than you did before; you see more in you than there was before."

Clifton Fadiman

You could reread the same classic every decade, and something seemingly new would jump out at you each time. Perhaps the first time you read *War and Peace,* you were most interested in the relationship between Pierre and Hélène. The next time you read it, you related more strongly to Prince Andrei and Natasha's romance. The next time, you were touched by Nikolai and Princess Marya. Classics are classics because they are masterpieces with a multitude of facets; it is impossible to grasp them all in one reading. People will be studying the classics for generations to come.

Today I will begin rereading a favorite classic.

Mine Eyes Have Seen the Glory

*"If the world shall disappoint you,
it will be your own fault."*

Mark Hopkins

What disappoints us each day? Bad traffic? Long lines? Defective machines? What things disappoint us in the world as a whole? Poverty? War? Natural disasters? The world does need improvement, but our outlook needs revision as well. We cannot expect things to go perfectly because just as we are not perfect, the world is not perfect. Instead of letting obstacles break our spirits, we must grow to expect hurdles; we need to see them as mere challenges on our path and find innovative solutions to overcome them. It is helpful to focus on the beautiful while working to change as much of the imperfect as possible.

Today I will pay special attention to the beautiful and take the imperfect in stride.

The Ugly Green Thing

*"The greatest pleasure I know is to do a good action
by stealth, and to have it found out by accident."*

Charles Lamb

I bought "the ugly green thing" at a rummage sale
for 50 cents in the early '90s. It looked like a
pea-green house that some kid made out of plaster
at Brownie Camp. I presented it to my brother Joe
for his birthday. Five weeks later, he sent it to me
for *my* birthday. Six months later, I hid it in the
linen closet in his Kentucky home. A year later,
I found it at the bottom of the woodpile in my
Milwaukee home. The object went back and forth
for years.

Once, Joe filled it with cement so it would be
prohibitively expensive for me to mail it back to
him. I once decorated it with a picture of Joe in
front, complete with a goofy hat and teeth. We've
added sayings, stickers, and each other's addresses
over the years. When I was a struggling single
parent, my finances were tight, and times were
tough; every time I found the ugly green thing,
however, I'd laugh for days, then giggle my way
through figuring out a devilish way to get it back
to Joe.

I once wrapped the object in freezer paper and put it at the bottom of the freezer chest in Joe's garage. A couple of years passed before he found it that time. Another time—while he and his wife were visiting me—I carefully hid the beast at the bottom of a huge tool chest in the back of his truck. The next morning they left to drive back to Kentucky, and I was quite sad. My spirits were lifted an hour later, however, when I stepped outside. There on the bench next to my front door sat the ugly green thing. Untold hours of laughter and storytelling have flowed from the green creature that just keeps on giving.

Today I will do a good action by stealth. It will bring joy into the recipient's life as well as my own.

Take Care of Yourself

"You have to expect things of yourself before you can do them."

Michael Jordan

When we are young and the adults in our life are tough on us, it can be confusing. As we have more experiences under our belts, though, we are grateful that things are expected of us. Everyone wants to contribute, and this is how we learn. We are given duties, and there are consequences when we fall short. We begin to know what we are capable of, and we push ourselves and expect things of ourselves as well. We are eventually capable of great things.

Today I will challenge myself. Perhaps I will push myself to try a different workout. Pilates, anyone?

Trying Every Which Way

*"If we knew what it was we were doing,
it would not be called research, would it?"*

Albert Einstein

*M*ost of us are not naturals at things we've never done before. Who cares if we fall? Everybody falls sometimes. Just get back up and try again. Never be afraid to try something new. Never tried ice-skating? Most communities have marvelous rinks, and it is a delightful activity. Watch the other skaters for a while. They glide across the ice—first one foot, then the other. Get out there. Take it slow at first, and then you'll be on your way.

Today I will attempt something new. If I don't catch on right away, I will remind myself that first attempts are "research."

How to Make Good Decisions

"Enough experience will make you wise."

James R. Cook

There's a famous story about an older woman who was asked by a younger woman how she got to be so wise. The old woman replied: "Good decisions." The young woman asked how she learned to make good decisions. The old woman said: "Experience." The young woman asked how she got the experience. The old woman said: "Bad decisions."

Today I will stop beating myself up over past bad decisions. I will rejoice that so many of my bad decisions have come full circle and made me wiser.

I Want, Therefore I Will Make

*"Imagination is the beginning of creation.
You imagine what you desire; you will what you
imagine; and at last you create what you will."*

George Bernard Shaw

Karl Benz imagined a speedy, horseless carriage. He dreamed of a means of travel and daily transportation that didn't include massive amounts of hay and cities filled with horse manure. He desired it, imagined it, and created it. What do you desire? Is there a product, service, or opportunity that you don't have in your life that you'd like? Think about it, plan it, and create it.

Today I will ponder my desires and try to make progress on making them a reality. Perhaps I will come up with a way of sending a never-ending supply of popcorn through tubes to each seat in the theater. Wait and see.

November 23

Happy Thanksgiving

"Absence sharpens love, presence strengthens it."
Thomas Fuller

When we're separated from our loved ones, we feel a pang inside. Past experiences tend to come to mind, and we long to have those fun times again. If we're lucky enough to spend a great deal of time with family and friends, it is easy to start taking these times for granted. In the midst of merriment and mayhem, especially on Thanksgiving, I try to step away from yet another nibble of scrumptious food and take in the scene. I see kids playing games, adults fixing snacks, other grown-ups rehashing the latest great argument, some watching football, some giggling and thinking up jokes to play, and a few just relaxing. I love this scene. I can almost feel my heart expanding.

Today I will give thanks for all my loved ones and send warm vibes toward all those who feel alone on this celebratory day.

Dream a Little Dream

*"Dreaming is an act of pure imagination,
attesting in all men a creative power,
which if it were available in waking,
would make every man a Dante or Shakespeare."*

H. F. Hedge

We've all experienced the fun of waking up out of a goofy, complicated, out-of-this-world dream. We quickly jot it down or describe it to a loved one before we forget it. Such dreams can provide the fodder for great novels, plays, songs, or other works of art.

If I have an outrageous or amazing dream today, I will note it in my journal. Perhaps I can make something of it one day. Move over, Shakespeare.

November 25

Let the Sun Shine In

*"Keep your face to the sunshine and
you will not see the shadows."*

Helen Keller

For years I did not like the month of November. The weeks of gray skies would get to me. I had SAD (Seasonal Affective Disorder), and I needed sunshine. I was able to move to Florida, and my problem is solved. We can't all live in Florida, but we can keep our days sunny by focusing on the blessings in our lives instead of on the difficulties.

Today if I start feeling down, I will call to mind at least one good thing that has made me happy recently. If I have read a touching story or seen a fabulous painting or wondrous flower with my own eyes, I will ponder this to brighten my day.

Big Dreams, Gigantic Memories

*"As long as you're going to be
thinking anyway, think big."*

Donald Trump

My friend Winnie lives in China; she wrote me a fan letter once, and we became e-mail friends. She wanted me at her wedding. She wanted her college professor (who had moved to Japan) and her Indian friends at her wedding as well. It seemed crazy at first, but we all figured, *Why not?* Winnie thought big, and her dream came true.

Today I will work to put one of my big dreams into motion. Perhaps I'll fill out the 15-page application to be a contestant on *Survivor*. Why not?

A Glass Half Full

"One day, someone showed me a glass of water that was half full. And he said, 'Is it half full or half empty?' So I drank the water. No more problem."

Alexander Jodorowsky

An optimist sees the glass as half full, a pessimist sees it as half empty, and a realist goes on with life instead of analyzing the glass. It is best to be a person of action rather than analyzing all day, but we also need to be mindful of our outlook; this way, we are sure to stay in the positive area of the slope.

Today I will endeavor to be a realistic optimist.

A Little Posh Is Good

"Whatever is worth doing at all is worth doing well."
Earl of Chesterfield

*M*ost of us have few times in our modern lives that call for simple elegance. Now and then I invite a group of loved ones over for dinner, and I thrive on these evenings. For more casual gatherings, I get a kick out of letting one of the little ones help me by setting the table. Sure, the utensils, glasses, and napkins end up scattered with no rhyme or reason, but who cares? The little ones will get it in time.

For my elegant gatherings, I enjoy planning a delicious sit-down dinner using the good plates, cloth napkins, a lovely tablecloth, knives (turned inward) to the right of the plates, spoons next to the knives, forks to the left of the plates. Drinking glasses are above the knives and spoons, and salad plates are above the forks. A table like this begs for pleasant, stimulating conversation. A special dinner is worth doing well.

Today I will plan a festive dinner with loved ones. All my guests will feel appreciated, partly because of the elegant table setting.

November 29

Too Bad, So Sad

"You cannot prevent the birds of sadness from flying over your head, but you can prevent them from nesting in your hair."

Chinese Proverb

It's okay to be sad. We all feel down from time to time. Sometimes we need a little sad. If we lose a loved one or suffer some other loss, it is natural to feel down for a while. We retreat to our rooms, look at old photos, and work through our loss. Sad happens—let it. Just don't let it last too long. If you can't seem to shake your sadness, get help. There's no shame in admitting that you are having difficulty. We all need help at times. Your loved ones will be relieved if you seek the help you need to pull you through this difficult time.

If I feel a little sad today, I will let myself wallow for a little while. After that little while passes, though, I will do something to distract myself from my grief. Perhaps I'll take a walk, go see a movie or exhibit, or phone a good friend.

Give It Away

"If you will think about what you ought to do for other people, your character will take care of itself."

Woodrow Wilson

Many of us spend a great deal of time pondering our character and fretting over what others think of us. It is true that if we just do what we know we ought to do all the time, we do not have to waste one moment worrying about our character. It is impossible to have bad character if we spend a good portion of our time helping others. We would all like to be philanthropists (wouldn't it be nice to have so much money we could give 95 percent of it away?), but since most of us have only limited incomes, we need to be creative in giving of ourselves. Most of us do have a sizable amount of free time. If—instead of always spending our free time on entertainment—we could spend some of it at a soup kitchen or with a child or a lonely elderly person, this would do wonders for others and for our own character.

Today I will offer to take an elderly neighbor to run errands.

December 1

Put Your Talents to Use

"Use what talents you possess; the woods would be silent if no birds sang except those that sang best."

Henry Van Dyke

I took six years of piano lessons, but I still cannot play well. When an occasion creeps up, I have to practice before I can play anything—and even then my timing is usually off. My false pride prevents me from playing in front of others unless I am pressured into it. Lately, though, I have been thinking that the folks in the nursing home down the street might appreciate a little music this time of year—even by an imperfect pianist. Time to swallow my pride, dust off the old music, and make merry.

Today I will not let pride keep me from shining.

Frugal Times Ten

"Whatever you have, spend less."
Samuel Johnson

f we live within our means, life is less stressful. This means delaying gratification, but it is worth it. We can save a certain amount of every paycheck for those bigger purchases. When we clip coupons and delay purchases, the difference between wants and needs become clearer to us, and decisions become easier. By the time we have enough money, we may even realize we don't even need that pricey car or other big purchase anymore.

I will not spend one more dime than I need to today.

Casting the First Stone

*"When a man points a finger
at someone else, he should remember that
four of his fingers are pointing to himself."*

Louis Nizer

Unless our actual job involves judging others, it is best to avoid this practice. Maybe we have heard rumors about the marital problems of our neighbors. Are we justified in treating them differently because of it? Not unless we have firsthand knowledge of a situation, and it is likely inappropriate even then. We would not consider it fair for someone to jump to conclusions about us for a circumstance we have little, if any, control over. Of course we can't help but have things go through our minds about others; we just need to be careful about saying much or accusing anyone. None of us is perfect, and thinking that we are superior to others is as questionable as nearly any other behavior.

If I am tempted to judge someone today, I will remind myself of some recent questionable behavior of my own, and I will bite my tongue.

Revenge Is a No-Win Enterprise

*"Before you embark on a journey
of revenge, dig two graves."*
Confucius

When we feel hurt, it is common to desire revenge. The problem, however, is that if you strike in revenge, your target will likely want revenge in return; soon the cycle gets completely out of hand, and the situation can even become dangerous. Both individuals end up spending ridiculous amounts of time and energy on something that likely would have taken minutes (okay, maybe hours) to resolve in a constructive fashion. Talk things out with the individual who wronged you. If one of you is not of the appropriate mind-set at the time, walk away for a while or get a willing, unbiased acquaintance involved. Constructive resolution will allow both of you to move on to better, more interesting things.

If anyone wrongs me today, I will not give in to any longing for revenge.

Yay or Nay, It's Up to You

"The optimist proclaims that we live in the best of all possible worlds, and the pessimist fears this is true."

James Branch Cabell

My friend Jack claims to be neither an optimist nor a pessimist. "I'm a realist," he says. "Things are what they are; some things are good, others are bad." Well, that's Jack's view, but I am definitely an optimist.

Optimists see struggles in life as mere challenges. Raising four children on my own made me strong, well-rounded, and more forgiving. It forced me to use my meager earnings creatively. I didn't choose that lifestyle, but once it was my reality, I struggled to focus on hope. It was not easy, but I came to figure it out to a point where I was even able to write two books about the experience. My goal was to pass some hope on to others who were facing similar struggles.

We all need to fight against pessimism. Pessimists are no fun to be around; they complain a lot and feel cheated in life. They waste their time wishing things were different and dreaming of things that will probably never happen. They have lost their perspective, and this is a dangerous, delusional thing. Why not spend your days marveling at the beauty around you every day instead?

We live in an interesting, exquisite world. If you haven't been to the places you've seen on postcards, make plans to go see them, even if you can't afford to go until next year or the year after that. Seeing these marvels firsthand will change you. If you feel pessimistic because you can't find beauty anywhere around you, save up and move. If your work keeps you in the dumps, figure out what kind of work would make you happier, and try to change jobs. Optimists focus on hope, and hope is real—it is not an illusion. There is always hope, and it is powerful. It can pull you out of the direst circumstances.

Today I will focus on hope and beauty.

Another Day, Another Notch

"My favorite thing is to go where I've never been."
Diane Arbus

We all have our favorite haunts, but we also need to make time to experience new places. This expands our minds and can be good for our spirits. What are we afraid of? That the new place will be awful? If so, we just won't go again, and it's just as likely it will be a wonderful experience—perhaps we will meet new friends or the new place will make its way onto our list of hot spots. This is, after all, how we discovered our favorite haunts in the first place.

Today I will do something that varies from my normal routine.

Dreaming of a Better World

*"Every great dream begins with a dreamer.
Always remember, you have within you the
strength, the patience, and the passion to
reach for the stars to change the world."*

Harriet Tubman

One of the tenets of civilized societies is that all individuals are created equal, and it follows that anyone can change the world. Think of all those before us who realized great changes for the world: Abraham Lincoln, Martin Luther King Jr., and Mother Teresa. The struggles they faced gave them the character and strength to pursue their dreams.

Today I will think of a way to help change the world. Perhaps I will start volunteering at a shelter in my community. Maybe I will run the shelter one day or start my own nonprofit.

What If?

*"The only way to discover the limits of the possible
is to go beyond them to the impossible."*

Arthur C. Clarke

What if all the medical professionals stopped researching new procedures because they decided our standard treatments were the best ones possible? We need to test the limits—otherwise we'll never learn anything. If the new techniques don't work, we can just go back to the tried-and-true way. But we should always be ready to try something new—once in a while we'll stumble upon a superior method or make a fantastic discovery.

If I feel curious about something new today, I will go for it. I will not be afraid.

One Big, Interesting World

*"To know when one's self is interested is the
first condition of interesting other people."*

Walter Pater

Think back over the speeches you've heard.
Some are memorable, while others are
forgettable. What makes a speech memorable? One
thing I've noticed is that if a speaker does not seem
inspired by his or her subject, I am sure to lose
interest quickly. But if the subject of his or her
speech lights up the speaker, I find myself getting
excited about the topic as well. What inspires you?
I find the people at the farmers' market inspiring.
There's the honey man, the man selling spicy dill
pickles, and the woman who gives out free canvas
bags but makes us sign a pledge that we will
use them instead of plastic bags. Their passion is
inspiring.

**Today I will reflect upon what inspires me, and I
will try to inspire others as well.**

Anticipation

"A promise is a cloud; fulfillment is rain."

Arabian Proverb

The anticipation of an adventure is often even more fun than the actual event. Sometimes the anticipation can be so delicious that it occupies our minds for weeks beforehand. I always told my children way in advance about almost everything we did—a bike ride or a picnic, a trip to the beach or to the circus, or a family vacation. I wanted them to get excited, to look forward to the activity, and plan for it. The anticipation added to the fun and almost seemed to lengthen our excursion.

Today I will plan a get-together with some friends. I will tell them about it now, so the anticipation can begin.

The Eye of the Creator

"Originality is simply a pair of fresh eyes."

Thomas Wentworth Higginson

When you visit an art museum, do you find yourself marveling at some paintings but being baffled by others? I have thought some seemed so simple, anyone could have created them. "I could have done that with my eyes closed," I've found myself saying on more than one occasion. My daughter (who is an art professor) has helped me realize that there are many different genres of art, and they don't all appeal to every visitor to a given museum. One visitor may go straight to the Impressionist gallery, while the next visitor makes a beeline for the modern wing. Some pieces depict specific scenes; others are more reactionary, and the inspiration for them may not be obvious at first. Just because it's not what I'm used to seeing doesn't mean it doesn't have value.

Today I will endeavor to have fresh eyes, and I will not make quick judgments.

The Whirling Dervish

*"There are people that want to be everywhere
at once, and they get nowhere."*

Carl Sandburg

*D*o you ever have days where you have countless tasks in mind, and you're so anxious to get them finished that you find yourself trying to do all of them at once? I flit from room to room, starting things, but never quite finishing anything. *Take it one step at a time.* That's what I keep telling myself—*one project at a time.*

On this hustle-bustle December day, I will take time to enjoy at least one cup of afternoon tea.

Wants and Needs

"There are only two tragedies in life: one is not getting what one wants, and the other is getting it."

Oscar Wilde

We have to be careful about deciding what we want. Perhaps our dream is to be a movie star. This is a dream that works out for only a select group of people; for these types of dreams, it is best to have an alternate plan. We can work at a restaurant while we take classes and go out on auditions. This way, we are following our heart, but we will not despair if our dream does not come to fruition. Perhaps our destiny is to be a proficient restaurant manager. Or, to take another example, what if our goal is to simply get rich? Maybe we end up achieving this goal but also step on our family members and all prospective friends in the process. We achieve our goal, but we likely end up unhappy, nonetheless.

I will take stock of my goals and dreams today and decide if they are worthwhile. If they are not, I will try to come up with new ones.

For Those Who Come After Us

"Your descendants shall gather your fruits."

Virgil

Do you ever find yourself wondering what it is all for? Perhaps you toil all day but never see concrete results. Many times, the fruits of our labors are not apparent until after we are gone. At the time of Martin Luther King Jr.'s assassination, his work was not accomplished, but his work was not in vain. We have gathered the fruits of his labor, and future generations will continue to do so.

Today I will think about my work. If it seems clearly only of use in the here and now, I will consider a career change or take up a fulfilling hobby.

Time for Joy

"Time you enjoyed wasting is not wasted time."

T. S. Eliot

All of our endeavors do not seem equal. Time spent working on the problems that plague the world does not seem equal to time spent on entertainment. But most of our endeavors do have merit—we just need to balance them. Take the ways we spend our time preparing for and enjoying the holidays. Some call these weeks "the silly season." Some of it may be truly silly and we can overdo it, but this time strengthens our bonds with others and recharges us for the coming year.

Today I will enjoy the spirit of the season.

Changing the Holidays

"Don't count the days, make the days count."

Muhammad Ali

When I was a kid, we used an Advent calendar to count down the days until Christmas. I still take part in the fun tradition with my grandkids, but I treasure each minute, while my grandkids just want these days to be over already.

I endeavor to make today count. I will donate gifts to a homeless shelter in my community to make sure the children who live there will be touched by the joy of the holidays this year.

Make Amends

A stiff apology is a second insult…
The injured party does not want to be compensated
because he has been wronged;
he wants to be healed because he has been hurt.

G. K. Chesteron

Apologies are not easy or fun, so most of us put them off. Often when we finally give them, we mumble and avoid eye contact. We've all had people apologize to us in this fashion, and it just does not work. Be genuine! Smile! Hug them or take their hand. Look them in the eye and just say, "I'm sorry! I know I messed up! Can you find it in your heart to forgive me? What will it take?" This time of year is perfect for apologies. We are in good cheer, anyway, so they come easier. And in this day and age—with Facebook and other networking sites—we can find nearly anyone we would ever want to apologize to. Once it's over, you'll be relieved, and your holidays will be all the merrier.

Today I will reflect on my relationships; if any need mending, I will seek out my loved one.

Do Whatever It Takes

*"When you come to the end of your
rope, tie a knot and hang on."*

Franklin D. Roosevelt

We humans have an amazing capacity to live through stress. We have thick skin and a fire deep in our gut that keeps us from giving up. But this time of year, many people feel stretched thin. We shop too much, bake too many cookies, send too many cards, and plan too many parties. Forget about perfect—make it fun. Instead of hosting a huge family dinner on Christmas, plan a more informal gathering at a central location and ask everyone to sign up to bring some component of the meal. When you feel like you're at the end of your rope, phone a friend, go for a walk, or read over some words that have inspired you in the past. You will soon feel invigorated once again.

Tonight I will not think about my to-do list. I will have a bubble bath, a cup of cocoa, and relax.

Zing, Zang, Zoom!

"Nothing great was ever achieved without enthusiasm."

Ralph Waldo Emerson

*E*nthusiasm is one of my favorite words. If we can muster enthusiasm for a task, that's half the battle. If we do something with enthusiasm—rather than just shuffling along—we can get the task done in half the time. Enthusiasm is a must over the holidays. It keeps us in the spirit of the season, and it helps make the year a memorable one.

I will muster enthusiasm for everything I do today, whether it's taking a friend to the airport or boogying down at a holiday party.

The Best Time of the Year

*"The great man is the one who does
not lose his child's heart."*

Mencius

What is your child's heart? It is your heart as it was during your first moments of life. It is innocent and true—it has never been broken or known sadness, and it thus has no reason to feel jaded or bitter. It is full of wonder, joy, and love for everyone and everything in its sphere. We can summon that heart again, can't we? We can let go of all the things that brought us down during the past year, and we can reflect on the many wonderful experiences. We can focus on the things that bring us together rather than on the trivial things that drive us apart. We can use these joyful feelings to grow closer to loved ones and start the coming year on the right foot.

Today I will summon my child's heart.

The World Beyond

"Imagination will often carry us to worlds that never were. But without it, we go nowhere."
Carl Sagan

*O*ur imaginations can come up with wild, fanciful things. Think of the world of Harry Potter: It was created out of the mind of an imaginative writer. But our imaginations can also help us solve everyday problems. Think of Post-it notes—they solve a seemingly small problem, but they improve our everyday lives.

Today I will use my imagination, whether it's for spicing up a recipe or inventing a world of polka-dot fairies for a future book.

Taking Mistakes in Stride

"The cleverest of all, in my opinion, is the man who calls himself a fool at least once a month."

Fyodor Dostoyevsky

When we feel foolish, our first instinct is to shrink back. A more constructive reaction, though, is to take it in stride. It is hard to learn something new without feeling foolish. Stepping out of our comfort zone strengthens us.

If I feel foolish today, I will remind myself that feeling foolish for a little while is better than never learning anything new.

Helping Those in Need

"At this festive season of the year…it is more than usually desirable that we should make some slight provision for the poor and destitute, who suffer greatly at the present time.…We choose this time, because it is a time, of all others, when Want is keenly felt, and Abundance rejoices."

Charles Dickens

The holidays are for sharing moments with and acknowledging our loved ones, but this is also an appropriate time to remember that there are many among us who have had some tough breaks. The holidays are perfect for giving these individuals a boost, as there are not many things in life more difficult than seeing joy all around you while feeling cast aside and forgotten. It is a fortunate thing to find ourselves in a position to help others in need.

Today I will make sure that in the hustle and bustle of this special season, I have not forgotten to give in some way to someone in my community who is unable to reciprocate. If my finances are slim at this point in my life, I will give of my time in some way instead.

December 24

A Treasured Possession

"There is no delight in owning anything unshared."
Seneca

One of my most treasured possessions is a delicate hand-painted wooden ball the size of an orange. Inside that ball is a smaller one, and so forth—twelve balls in all. My dad's oldest sister gave him this set in 1925, when he was six years old. The price ($1.00) is written in pencil inside the largest ball. I love to get the set out and delight my grandchildren by opening it, one ball at a time, and watching their eyes glisten. When the set sits in the cupboard, it just sits. But when it's on the table amazing little eyes, it's a treasure come to life.

Today I will look through my belongings and find something I've been saving for "a special occasion"—maybe a fancy set of dishes or a fine wine. I will share my treasure with loved ones before this year ends.

A Miraculous Day

"...all is a miracle. The stupendous order of nature, the revolution of a hundred million worlds around a million stars, the activity of light, the life of all animals, all are grand and perpetual miracles."

Voltaire

On this day, it is easy to look around us and see everything as a miracle: the crisp air; the lights that cast a magnificent glow on our neighborhoods; and the fact that at this time of year, we are able to put our differences aside and send good tidings near and far. Most of the basis for this season flows from a humble being who was love personified, which makes this season all the more magnificent.

Today I will revel in the joy that surrounds me.

December 26

The Simple Life

"I have lived through much and now I think I have found what is needed for happiness. A quiet, secluded life in the country with the possibility of being useful."

Leo Tolstoy

It is difficult for most of us in the modern world to live the simple life. Our society involves trade through money, and for money we need to work, which means most of us live in cities near our workplaces. But if we keep our lives as simple as possible, time does not escape us so quickly.

Today I will live simply. I will enjoy the quiet of the early morning, and I will avoid multitasking, if possible.

Beauty in Unlikely Places

"It isn't hard to love a town for its greater and lesser towers, its pleasant parks or its flashing ballet. Or for its broad and bending boulevards...But you never truly love it till you can love its alleys too."

Nelson Algren

It's easy to love the obvious positive elements of a place—or of a person, for that matter. It's harder to love the darker, hidden areas, but those areas usually have strong points as well. Alleys are utilitarian; they house the garbage cans and other unsightly but necessary elements. By doing so, they enable us to put up a good front. Alleys are not beautiful, but they play their part, and city dwellers grow to appreciate them. In a similar fashion, we grow to love the hidden aspects of our loved ones. We treasure these aspects because few are acquainted with them. We are honored that our loved ones trust us enough to share them with us.

If I start to make a flip judgment about something today, I will try to find its beauty or usefulness.

Memory Making

"It's a pleasure to share one's memories. Everything remembered is dear, endearing, touching, precious. At least the past is safe—though we didn't know it at the time. We know it now. Because it's in the past; because we have survived."

Susan Sontag

Around this time, many of us love to reminisce about the events of the past year. It's fun to relive the good times and marvel at how we've changed and grown. Even if what happened wasn't so great, we can reflect on what we learned from the experience and be glad that it is in the past. Somehow time has a way of making the past seem not so bad after all. The memories take on a *Leave It to Beaver* feel, and we appreciate all of the events as having contributed to forming our present circumstances.

Today I will make time for reminiscing or looking through old albums with a loved one.

Pssst! Pass It On!

"When we do the best we can, we never know what miracle is wrought in our life, or in the life of another."

Helen Keller

Imagine the possibilities. If you write one letter to one prisoner, maybe your kind words will bring hope to his or her life. Or let's say you tell one person a funny story. They repeat it to six friends, and the ripple effect brings a smile to many faces.

Today I will pass something on. Perhaps I will make a pot of homemade soup and give half to my elderly neighbor. Who knows, maybe she'll pass some of it on and bring joy to even more people.

December 30

Stand Tall

"We know what happens to people who stay in the middle of the road. They get run over."

Aneurin Bevan

Many of us do feel safer being "middle-of-the-road" people. Being on one side or the other can lead to confrontation, and many of us prefer to avoid that. Wouldn't standing up for something give our lives more meaning, though? Isn't there something you feel passionate about—a topic that comes up that makes you feel something, even if you aren't sure why? We need to analyze these seemingly unprompted feelings, for they hint at our deepest convictions. What are we afraid of? That we might offend someone or look stupid? Standing up for what we believe in shouldn't offend anyone if we do it with grace and compassion, and it shouldn't make us look stupid if we are simply engaged in a tactful discussion about ideas.

Today I will not be afraid to take a stand.

Wind in Our Wings

"God provides the wind, but man must raise the sails."
Augustine of Hippo

Sometimes we want (or even expect) a miracle. We want to find the perfect job. We want the bills to go away. We want less stress, more money, fewer responsibilities, and better relationships. The wind for all of this is here—it is all around us. There are job opportunities around every corner—we just have to seek them out. Are any of them our ideal position? Maybe, maybe not. Maybe one of them will lead to our dream job. We can make the bills go away and have less stress, more money, and fewer responsibilities by sacrificing and making good decisions. We can have better relationships by improving our communication skills and—again—making good decisions. We have the knowledge and the raw materials to achieve our dreams. It will just take a little work and dedication on our part. Life is not easy, but when we do the work, the ship sails beautifully.

Today I will hold up my end of the bargain. I will get to work.